QUICKSTART

YOUR

QUICKBOOKS

A COMPREHENSIVE BEGINNER'S GUIDE
TO WORKING WITH QUICKBOOKS ONLINE

Ronika Khanna CPA, CA, CFA

Disclaimer

The author of this book and the accompanying materials has used their best efforts in preparing this book. The author makes no representation or warranties with respect to the accuracy, applicability, fitness, or completeness of the contents of this book. The information contained in this book is strictly for educational purposes. Therefore, if you wish to apply ideas contained in this book, you are taking full responsibility for your actions.

CONTENTS

TO THE READER

Complimentary PDF Version with Links

Throughout this book there are links to various resources that do not appear in the print version. If you would like a complimentary version of the PDF with links, please email me at ronika@montrealfinancial.ca along with proof of purchase, and I would be happy to send it to you.

Reviews and Feedback

If you find this book useful, I would greatly appreciate a testimonial or review on the website where you purchased it.

Alternatively, if you think the book doesn't address certain issues or you are left with lingering questions, I would very much like to hear about that as well.

You can leave your comments directly on my website by completing my feedback form or send me an email at ronika@montrealfinancial.ca.

INTRODUCTION

Over the years, I have used QuickBooks Desktop and QuickBooks Online extensively in my accounting practice. As an accountant that specializes in small business, it was important to find a software that was user friendly for business owners since many of my clients do their own accounting. Over the years, I have been impressed with the functionality of QuickBooks and ongoing improvements that help businesses to streamline their accounting, save time and get financial insights. Best of all, anyone with a little time and effort can learn to use QuickBooks without needing an accounting degree.

As QuickBooks has evolved, more and more resources have been devoted to improving the online product. While the desktop version is still very powerful, the majority of business owners want to be able to access their accounting from anywhere—including their smartphones--which is much easier when your data is on the internet. Consequently, my own practice has started to focus more on the online version.

The goal of this book is to introduce you to QuickBooks Online (hereinafter referred to as QBO) and to walk you through the steps of using it as effectively as possible. I have trained numerous small business owners on how to use QBO and have found the methodology used in this book to be the most effective in understanding how QBO works and the learning the functionality that every new business should know.

While this book can be read chapter by chapter, it also serves as a reference when you require an explanation relating to a specific task.

This book contains 3 distinct parts:

QBO Overview

In the first section, I provide a broad overview of QBO including:

- Features available in QBO.
- General accounting and QBO-specific terminology that every business owner should know.
- Different versions of QBO.
- What to consider when you already have an accounting file.
- Signing up for the first time.

- Best practices and common mistakes
- Navigating the main interface of QBO.

Once you're familiar with the basics, it's time to make QBO your own.

QBO Customization

The second section relates to the setup and customization of your file in QBO. As you will discover, QBO has a plethora of features that you should familiarize yourself with. Most of the setup is accomplished through the various menus that are available via the ⚙ **Gear icon**. I take you through each set up option including:

- Details relating to your business.
- Sales and expense customization.
- Adding users.
- Customizing invoices.
- Setting up the Chart of Accounts.
- Setting up product and service details.
- Connecting bank and credit card accounts.
- Setting up sales tax tracking.

Once setup, these menus will only be needed occasionally when you have to change something.

QBO Day to Day

The final section relates to the day-to-day functionality of QBO and is focussed on the **Left-hand Navigation Bar**. This includes:

- Invoicing and receiving payments from customers.
- Processing transactions from suppliers.
- Downloading and processing banking transactions.
- Reviewing and generating reports.
- Filing sales tax returns.
- Preparing Journal entries.

NAVIGATING THIS BOOK

This book uses a number of conventions in order to best help you match the information and procedures presented with QuickBooks Online's user inferface. Most of the action terms, like "click", "select", "enter" are familiar. Here are some visual cues that are new:

Commands and Features

- **Bold text** indicates a feature in QBO. Sometimes it is simply a name or label, but most often this is something that you will interact with.

- **<Button>** is something that you click on to perform a discrete action, like **<Save>**. QBO has a number of buttons that combine with a dropdown. Clicking **<Save▼ >** will open a dropdown menu containing several options. In the case of a split button, e.g., **<Save| ▼ >**, clicking the command will perform that action while clicking the down arrow ▼ will allow open the dropdown menu.

- ▼ indicates a dropdown menu. This may be a field, a button, or another feature.

- Dropdown menu items are indicated thus.

- **>** This arrow appears next to some **Left-hand Navigation Bar** items and indicates a slide-out submenu. Often, those submenu items take you directly to a **[Tab]** on that items interface.

- ☑ indicates a checkbox. Checkboxes allow you to select multiple items, and sometimes select features that activate additional options.

- ⊙ indicates a radio button. Radio buttons are used to select one of a series of mutually exclusive options.

- → indicates the order of commands in a menu or series of menus. For example, the command to create a new Invoice using the **<+ New>** button and then select **Invoice** from the menu that then opens would appear as follows:

- Click **<+ New>** → **Invoice**.

- **[Tab]**   will switch your view to one of a series of pages all linked to the same task you are performing. The **Dashboard**, for example, has two tabs:

- **[Get things done] [Business overview]**

- Essentials **and/or** Plus **only**   indicates that a feature is only available at a particular subscription level.

Icons

- ⚙ **Gear icon**   opens an important menu panel for accessing numerous features. This book contains a comprehensive exploration of this part of QBO.

- ✏ **Pencil icon**   will unlock a set of fields, toggles, etc that allow you to change how QBO works and what information is set to default.

Text Boxes

Sometimes, it is useful to illustrate QBO's functionality using examples.

> ❖   An **EXAMPLE** box illustrates the result of a procedure, a case study, or an illustration.

In addition, there are a number of different commentary boxes throughout the book.

> ⚠   An **ALERT** box contains a warning.

> ➢   A **NOTE** box contains a comment or a point for consideration.

> ⚡   An **OPTION** box provides an alternative way to navigate to this feature.

> ✓   A **TIP** box suggests a way to work more efficiently or effectively.

Also see the chapter on Navigating QBO.

PART 1: QBO OVERVIEW

WHAT IS QUICKBOOKS ONLINE AND HOW CAN IT HELP YOU?

All businesses, without exception, require some form of accounting. If you have a very small business or very few transactions, you might choose to use a spreadsheet, while the more old-fashioned might opt for a handwritten ledger book. There are also some business owners who forego an accounting system altogether and do their calculations, as the saying goes, on the back of an envelope.

There does come a point for many businesses when these methods are no longer sufficient, while other businesses require a proper accounting solution right from the outset. The right accounting solution is the one that adds value to your business at a price point that makes sense.

There are numerous accounting software but perhaps none more popular than QuickBooks. They have both a desktop solution, which you install and use on your computer, and an online solution, which is accessible from any device via an internet connection, i.e., in the cloud. QBO has been gaining in popularity over the past few years and many businesses have transitioned over from QuickBooks Desktop (QBDT) largely due to QBO's advanced functionality and the ability to connect from anywhere.

Benefits of QBO

QBO possesses most of the features that a good accounting software should have and more functionality is being added as adoption of QBO continues to grow.

Cost

One of the most attractive aspects of QuickBooks Online (QBO) is you get a fully functional accounting software at a relatively low cost. There are several alternative pricing plans, depending on your needs, starting at $20 per month for the most basic plan. There are usually discounts for the first three months that allow you to test the software and ensure that it adequately meets your requirements. While a monthly subscription isn't free and can add up over time, I usually ask my clients to consider how much their time is worth. If your time is better spent working on your business, and you are able to save an hour or more per month by using software rather than a spreadsheet or a ledger book, then it makes sense to use it. Conversely, if your business is very simple and you already have a system that works for you, then making the change might not be worth the investment.

Size of Your Business and Complexity

QBO is ideal for and primarily marketed towards small businesses. There are no hard and fast rules about how big your business is before QBO is no longer suitable; however, if you have thousands of transactions per month, you might require additional functionality that QBO is unable to provide, along with performance issues. QBO does not impose any limits on file size or number of transactions. The only notable limits are with respect to character limits in fields, size limits when exporting a report to Excel, and technical issues that can slow your QuickBooks Online experience. A full list of limits can be found here.

Businesses that have more complex requirements might find QBO to be limited in its functionality. For example:

- **Sales orders** are not built into QBO. The alternative is to use "Estimates" which is similar but not exactly the same, especially if you are used to using sales orders. Another option is to use one of a number of third-party apps that integrate with QBO to provide sales orders functionality.
- **Inventory tracking** is limited in QBO. If your Inventory needs are complex, you can still use QBO along with a third-party app or you might have to consider another software.
- **Multiple companies** cannot be consolidated in QBO. However, once again there are apps that can help you accomplish this. Additionally, if you have several small holding companies, you could obtain a monthly subscription for each, but this can become costly.

Online/Cloud Access

Being able to access your information anytime and anyplace is becoming essential for small business owners. QBO by definition is accessible online and also has a mobile app where many of the day-to-day accounting functions can be performed and is included with your subscription. Of course, this means that you must be online to use QBO.

Banking

One of the most significant time saving features of QBO is its ability to connect with most banks and download your business bank and credit card data daily. Once you have set up a separate bank account for your business, the amount of time spent on simple data entry is reduced significantly as transaction details are downloaded and can be categorized directly from the **[Banking tab]**. QBO also saves time on bank reconciliations, and you can, at a glance, know if your accounts are reconciled by comparing the balance per QBO vs the bank balance found on the **[Banking tab]** (assuming all transactions from the banking download are entered). QBO allows you to create rules for transactions that occur regularly. You can assign sales taxes, Classes and Locations, and customer/supplier names directly within the **Banking** interface. You can also "split" transactions into more than one account and assign separate tax codes to each part of the split transaction.

Sales Tax

QBO handles GST/HST and PST (for provinces that have their own sales tax in addition to GST) with ease. You can set up sales tax rates that apply to each province. Once the set up is complete, you are prompted to apply sales tax codes to each transaction, including invoices, expenses, bills, and even journal entries. When you are ready to file your sales tax, you can access the report, which can be generated by period and breaks down the taxes payable by the line numbers (fields) that are on the Revenue Canada (CRA) GST/HST report and/or the Revenue Quebec (RQ) GST/HST and QST report. These can simply be transcribed and filed online using CRA *My Business Account* or RQ *My Account for businesses* or business online banking.

Payroll

If your business has employees, QBO has basic payroll functionality where you can set up employees and salaries. QBO will calculate your deductions at source (DAS) as well as generate your T4s (and RL1s if in Quebec) at year end. It should be noted that the DAS reporting, payments, and T4 slips, while generated by QBO, still have to be submitted to CRA manually. While QBO does an adequate job of doing the payroll, it is not the strongest feature, especially if your payroll is a bit more complex.

Invoicing and Customers

QBO allows you to enter Invoices that can then be sent via email or, if you are more traditional, via mail. While customization of Invoices templates is possible in QBO, there are limitations, mostly with respect to design. If the design of your Invoices is important to your business, you might want to consider a third-party invoicing software. Adding and customizing Customers in QBO is straightforward, and you can organize Customers into sub-Customers, which can be very useful when you have one main customer but several different branches or shipping Locations. There are also a variety of easily customizable reports available for your customer receivables and sales that can help you analyze your business.

Expenses and Vendors

Entering Expenses and Suppliers/vendors is straightforward. You can create the vendors and enter the Expenses in several different ways. Vendor reports provide you with various details about your Accounts Payable and Expenses.

Foreign Exchange

Having to deal with multiple currencies can be a frustrating experience. QBO has made significant strides in how foreign currency is integrated. Once this feature is activated, you can invoice Customers and enter Expenses in almost any currency you choose. It calculates the rates on the date of the transaction and creates a gain or loss for the difference in exchange rates between the invoice or bill date and the payment date. You can also easily calculate your unrealized gains and losses at the end of a period.

> ⚠ *Note that multicurrency cannot be turned off once activated.*

Credit Card Payments from Customers

There are a number of services such as Stripe and Paypal that allow you to accept credit card payments from Customers. You can also sign up to receive credit card payments directly with QBO at comparable rates. The advantage of doing so is that you can integrate a payment link directly onto your invoice that makes it very easy for Customers to pay your Invoices. Additionally, QBO handles the recording of payments so that no additional data entry is required.

Ease Of Use

While any accounting software has a learning curve, QuickBooks (online and desktop) has always been specifically designed for non-accountants. Many business owners who are using accounting software for the first time might not find it immediately intuitive; however, having trained many small business owners, it becomes easier (and even fun) over time. There are also numerous training resources provided by QBO and a large eco-system of third-party resources, including blog posts and videos, that can help you with issues as they arise.

Reports

QBO has numerous reports that allow you to gain insights and analyze your data. Financial Statements such as the Profit and Loss Statement, Balance Sheet, and Statement of Cash Flows provide a big picture view of your business, while Sales and Expense Reports allow you to drill down into your data and glean important insights. Every field in QBO has an associated report that can be queried and analyzed.

Add-ons and Apps

The advantage of being the most popular small business accounting software is that QBO has spawned an entire industry of supporting apps and add-ons that integrate seamlessly. There are hundreds of add-ons for QuickBooks that help manage Inventory, invoicing, point of sale systems, reporting, web stores, and a variety of other functions. Some of these help save time, such as OCR software that can read your bills and receipts and then import it directly into QBO. Other apps handle more complex accounting functions such as consolidation when you have multiple companies for which you want to see combined results and inventory when you need more functionality than QBO offers in its current version.

Import/Export to Excel/Google Docs

Most reports can be exported to Excel and Google Docs, which is great for manipulating data and creating reports in a variety of formats when QBO reports themselves are not sufficient. Importing data from Excel or Google Docs into QBO is not as flexible, as files have to be formatted very specifically and there are limitations on what can be imported. That said, QBO has expanded what can be imported from simple lists of Customers, vendors, and accounts in the past to Invoices and Bills now. There are also third-party apps that have significantly better integration functionality though often at a cost.

Security and Users

QuickBooks allows you to set security levels and user permissions so that only certain users can access certain modules. There are limitations on what data can be viewed, and it is quite easy to delete transactions and manipulate data compared with more sophisticated accounting software. However, QBO does have an audit trail report that reports on every transaction that is entered, modified, or deleted. As with any accounting software, it is important to ensure that you have good controls and processes in place, particularly if someone other than the business owner is using the system.

Having used QuickBooks extensively, I am often quite impressed with its functionality. It continues to improve every year and has some great features and flexibility that more sophisticated accounting software is often lacking.

ACCOUNTING TERMS THAT EVERY BUSINESS OWNER SHOULD KNOW

When starting your business, you will be subjected to a great deal of financial jargon. These terms are important to know with respect to QBO; you will have a better grasp of its functionality and be better able to navigate it comfortably. Additionally, you might be asked for financial information from your bank, CRA or RQ, Suppliers, Customers, and various other business partners. If you are unfamiliar with the terminology, then simple accounting and financial reporting becomes more difficult. Arming yourself with a basic vocabulary of the most common financial and accounting terms will help you develop a better understanding of your business and therefore be well equipped to answer any questions that come your way.

Accounts Receivable (A/R)

The accounting term for when Customers owe you money is Accounts Receivable. This is also referred to as Customers Receivables or simply by its acronym: AR. If you have an accounting software where you enter your Invoices to Customers and corresponding payments, you will be able to produce what is known as an AR Aging Summary, which is a report that lists all the amounts that Customers owe you, usually categorized in 30-day increments. The AR Aging Summary has the receivables that are the newest, referred to as current, in the first column. Each subsequent column is increased by 30 days i.e., current, 30 days, 60 days, 90 days, and then anything over 90 days is combined into one column. For example, a customer that you invoiced 2 months ago who has not yet paid you will show up under the 60 days heading. The older the accounts receivable, the more problematic it is, since there is a lower chance that it will be collected. It is important to know exactly which Customers owe you money at any given time and follow up with them regularly to increase the chances of being paid. Anyone analyzing your business, such as a bank that is determining if you are creditworthy, will assess the age of the receivables and assign a lower value to them. Accounts Receivable are a Current Asset on your Balance Sheet.

Accounts Payable (A/P)

Similar to accounts receivable, Accounts Payable refers to the list of suppliers to whom the business owes money. These may also be referred to as supplier or vendor payables. This report provides valuable information about how much you owe to your Suppliers and can provide insights as to when you should make payments, which can help with cash flow analysis. Accounts Payable are a Current Liability on the Balance Sheet.

Assets

Anything that your business owns or from which it expects to derive a future benefit is referred to as an asset. For example, the money in your bank or investment accounts are Assets. The equipment or machinery that is used to run your business, and the amounts that Customers owe you (Accounts Receivable) are also Assets. Assets are of three main types:

Current assets are available to you within the next year without restriction, such as cash in the bank or Inventory

Long term assets are restricted and are not readily available in the short term, such as an investment in another company, which usually cannot be sold immediately

Property, plant, and equipment represents tangible items such as computers, furniture, machinery etc.

Balance Sheet

The report that shows the assets, liabilities and equity of a business is referred to as a Balance Sheet. The reason it is called a Balance Sheet is that the assets will always equal the total of liabilities and equity due to the double entry system of accounting. This simply means that there are two sides to every transaction which are referred to as debits and credits that must be equal. This is one of the primary reports included in the Financial Statements.

Bill

When an individual or entity provides you with a product or service, they give you a document that provides details of the product or service and the amount payable. This is referred to as a Bill.

Budget or Forecast

When you want to predict your business performance over a specific period in the future, you will need to prepare a budget or a forecast. This is a very useful exercise for many business owners, even if only for their own purposes, as it allows them to see how they expect their businesses to perform. This can then be compared to their actual results and analysed to determine the reasons for the difference. You can use the Profit and Loss Statement as a template to predict your sales and Expenses for the coming year or for several years into the future. For more granularity, you can create a monthly budget. Many business owners find it difficult to make Estimates particularly when they are just starting their businesses, but as you accumulate history for your business, the process becomes simpler.

Chart of Accounts (COA)

A Chart of Accounts is the structural framework by which you summarize all the data that is entered into your accounting system. Each transaction that is entered is assigned to an account that is then condensed on an accounting report, such as the Profit and Loss Statement.

Cost of Goods Sold (COGS)

The direct costs of selling your product and sometimes services (if you have significant direct costs) are collectively referred to as Cost of Goods Sold. This will include costs to purchase the raw materials or items that you sell, packaging of your product, shipping and duties, labels etc. COGS also includes the cost of the labour to produce the goods.

Customer

An individual or business that buys your products or services. Can also be referred to as a client, particularly for service-based businesses.

Equity

When you deduct liabilities from your assets, the result is known as equity (or negative equity if your liabilities exceed your assets). Equity usually comprises the total contributions by the owner AND the accumulation of profits and losses since the inception of the company less any amounts withdrawn by the shareholders or owners in the form of direct withdrawals or dividends.

Expense

Costs that you incur that relate to your business and which are not included in Cost of Goods Sold are referred to as Expenses. These are usually indirect costs or overhead costs that must be incurred to run your business. For accounting and tax purposes, Expenses are categorized by type of Expense which you set up via your Chart of Accounts. Some of the more common Expense categories include:

- Salaries
- Rent
- Advertising and/or Marketing
- Office expenses

- Dues and subscriptions
- Travel
- Utilities
- Accounting and legal fees

Determining which Expense categories are most relevant will depend on the specific requirements of the business. Having meaningful Expense categories set up in your Chart of Accounts can provide a great deal of information and are especially useful for analysis.

Financial Statements

A typical Financial Statement comprises the following:

- Profit and Loss statement.
- Balance Sheet.
- Statement of cash flows.
- Notes to the Financial Statements, which provide details for some of the line items on the Financial Statements and are generally prepared by accountants at the year end depending on your mandate with the accountant.

Property, Plant, and Equipment (Fixed Assets) and Depreciation

Items that are purchased for the business, that will likely last for at least one year and possibly much longer, are referred to as Fixed Assets. These include machinery, equipment, computers, furniture, and improvements. This also includes intangible items that provide long term benefits such as a customer list or a brand name or a special software/app that are usually costly to create and will last for several years.

Accounting recognizes that when you purchase a fixed asset, it will not hold on to its value forever. Rather, the value of most assets diminishes with the passage of time. This reduction in value in accounting terms is known as Depreciation (also known as capital cost allowance for tax purposes). There are several methods of depreciation which can be used to capture the loss most accurately in the value of the asset.

Gross Margin (GM)

The difference between your total sales and Cost of Goods Sold is referred to as the Gross Margin. This is also often expressed as a percentage by dividing the gross margin dollar amount by the total sales. The gross margin gives you insights into the direct costs of selling your product and can be used as a comparison to other businesses in your industry and various other types of financial analysis including determination of your breakeven point.

Inventory

If you sell goods, you usually have items that you have on hand but have not yet sold. Inventory includes items that have either been purchased, but not yet assembled and/or items that are fully assembled and ready to be sold. Inventory is a current asset on your Balance Sheet.

Invoice

An invoice is a document, presented to a customer by you, that indicates the details about a service for which the customer then owes you payment at a specified date. Invoices can have a variety of details and most commonly include the date, invoice number (which is often sequential), product or service being sold, details about the product or service, quantity, price per unit, amount, sales tax if applicable, and the total including sales tax.

Liability

When your business owes money such as a loan to a bank or shareholder, or to Suppliers for purchase of goods or services, it is referred to as a liability. Like assets, these are also classified as current for amounts that are due within the next year or long term for amounts that are only due after one year or more. An amount due to a supplier or taxes payable to the government are usually current, while a bank loan that has a fixed term exceeding one year is long term.

Profit and Loss Statement (P&L)

A Profit and Loss Statement quite simply shows the sales, Cost of Goods Sold, and Expenses by category. The last line on the Profit and Loss Statement is either a net profit if sales exceed Expenses or a net loss when Expenses exceed sales.

The Profit and Loss Statement, which is also referred to as the income statement, is one of the most important (and most requested), reports for a business owner. It is used by banks to determine your suitability for a loan or credit and by the tax authorities to determine how much taxes you will pay. It also gives the business owner significant insights into how their business is doing and provides the data to identify areas that require improvements.

Retained Earnings (RE)/Owners' Equity

The accumulation of profits and losses, minus any dividends or distributions to shareholders, is referred to as retained earnings, which is a term that only applies to corporations. A sole proprietorship would simply reflect the accumulation of earnings as owner's equity on the Balance Sheet.

Sale

Anytime you sell a product or service or earn income for business purposes from another party e.g., a customer or client, it is referred to as a sale. From an accounting perspective, this is referred to as sales or revenues. There are conventional sales such as selling your cupcakes or web design services. Less conventional sales would include ad revenues from Google on your website or YouTube account, affiliate or referral commissions, or payments from a service such as Patreon or a Kickstarter/GoFundMe campaign. This also includes payments received in kind i.e., payments which are not received in the form of cash but a product or a free trip or subscription for which you would have to determine the fair market value and reflect them as sales.

Shareholder/Owner Loan

The term shareholder applies specifically to corporations (as structurally you can only own shares in a corporation) while the equivalent term for a sole proprietorship would simply be owner. Often shareholders will lend or borrow money from their businesses. If they lend money to a corporation, it means that the corporation must pay them back. This is referred to as a shareholder loan payable. Conversely, amounts borrowed by the shareholder from the corporation are referred to as shareholder loans receivable since the money is owed to the corporation. Shareholder loans may be treated similarly to a third-party loan where interest is charged and/or there are specific payment terms. It should be noted that shareholder loans that are receivable by a corporation (i.e., when a shareholder borrows money from a corporation) have tax consequences if not repaid within a specific period of time.

Statement of Cash Flows

The Profit and Loss Statement, while showing you the performance of the business, is not an accurate reflection of the cash that is generated or spent by the business. This is because the Profit and Loss Report includes sales and purchases made on credit (Accounts Receivable and Accounts Payable), depreciation and other items that have no impact on cash. There are many profitable businesses that have a negative cash flow or net cash outflows.

The statement of cash flows shows exactly how much net cash is spent or generated by a business. A typical cash flow statement separates cash flow into three categories:

- **Operating activities**, which breaks down the cash inflows and outflow relating to the regular operations of the business.
- **Investing activities**, which breaks down the cash inflows and outflow relating to investments made and sold.
- **Financing activities**, which breaks down the cash inflows and outflow from financing activities such as loans or equity

Supplier

An individual or business from whom you purchase products or services. Also referred to as a vendor.

WHICH VERSION OF QBO SHOULD YOU SELECT?

QBO like many software offers the option of either a free trial for 30 days or reduced pricing for a period of time. If you are reviewing several different accounting software it might make more sense to go with the free trial to give you time to experiment with each. However, if you are leaning towards using QBO then taking the discounted price for 3 months is the better value.

Currently, in Canada, QBO offers three version: EasyStart, Essentials, and Plus.

	MOST POPULAR	
EasyStart	**Essentials**	**Plus**
$20	$40	$60
$10/mo	**$20**/mo	**$30**/mo
Save 50% for 3 months*	Save 50% for 3 months*	Save 50% for 3 months*
Buy now	Buy now	Buy now
Includes:	Includes:	Includes:
✓ Track income & expenses	✓ Track income & expenses	✓ Track income & expenses
✓ Track sales & sales tax	✓ Track sales & sales tax	✓ Track sales & sales tax
✓ Capture & organize receipts	✓ Capture & organize receipts	✓ Capture & organize receipts
✓ Track mileage automatically	✓ Track mileage automatically	✓ Track mileage automatically
✓ Run reports	✓ Run reports	✓ Run reports
✓ Invoice & accept payments	✓ Invoice & accept payments	✓ Invoice & accept payments
✓ Progress invoicing	✓ Progress invoicing	✓ Progress invoicing
✓ Maximize tax deductions	✓ Maximize tax deductions	✓ Maximize tax deductions
✓ Send estimates	✓ Send estimates	✓ Send estimates
	✓ Multiple users	✓ Multiple users
	✓ Manage bills & payments	✓ Manage bills & payments
	✓ Multi-currency support	✓ Multi-currency support
	✓ Track time	✓ Track time
		✓ Track project profitability
		✓ Track inventory
Add-on	Add-on	Add-on

The version you choose depends on the specific features you might need. Below are some questions that will help you determine what version to choose:

Features Required	Version
Would you like to track Bills, which allows you to pay Suppliers at a later date and generate Accounts Payable reports?	Essentials
Do you need more than one user to access your file (not including an accountant)?	Essentials
Do you have Customers or Suppliers in other countries? And do you want to be able to invoice them or enter Bills or transactions in foreign currencies?	Essentials
Do you want to track time for yourself or employees?	Essentials
Do you sell products that require you to track Inventory?	Plus
Does your business have separate divisions or Locations or another metric for which you would like to generate Reports?	Plus
Do you want to prepare budgets for your business?	Plus
Do you have specific projects for which you would like to track profitability?	Plus

If you do not require any of the above features, you can sign up for the EasyStart version of QBO. Upgrading to a higher version as your business grows or the need for one or more of these features arise is very simple.

> ➢   *There is another version called "Self Employed" which is for very simple*
> *businesses. It should be noted that this version is not currently upgradeable*
> *to the versions listed above. Instead, a new file would have to be created*
> *and transactions and balances would have to be transferred manually.*

SIGNING UP FOR THE FIRST TIME

1. Once you have signed up for QBO, you will be prompted to enter some information about your business.

> ✓ *The information you enter can always be changed at a later date so don't be afraid to enter whatever information you think is most appropriate.*

Step 1 ❖ intuit **quickbooks**   SET UP YOUR QUICKBOOKS   1 of 4

1. Tell us about your business.

Everyone needs something a little different from QuickBooks. Let's get to know what you need so we can tailor things to fit you. You can change your info anytime in Settings.

Legal business name

Sherlock Holmes Detective Agency

How long have you been in business?

1-2 years   ⌄

Industry

Management, Consulting and Advertising Services   ⌄

Select the category that best describes what you do. Change this anytime in Settings.

☐ I want to bring in my data from QuickBooks Desktop, Sage 50 Desktop, Xero, or Excel

Next

- **Legal business name** is the name of your business.
- **How long have you been in business?** ▼ can be anywhere from less than 1 year to 15+ years.
- **Industry** ▼ is the type of business that most closely matches what is available in QBO's dropdown. QBO simply uses this to create a chart of accounts, so don't worry too much about setting up the exact business.

- ☑ **I want to bring in my data from QBDT, Sage 50 Desktop, Xero, or Excel** can be checked if you are intending to transition over. You will then be presented with another dropdown listing the accounting software that QBO can help import. This is an advanced topic and beyond the scope of this book.

Once you have completed the fields, click on **<Next>**.

2.   You will be taken to the following screen:

---

2. What's your role at your business?

We'll use this info to help personalize your QuickBooks. You can always change it later in Settings.

| Owner | Accountant | Employee | Bookkeeper |

It's something else

Do you have an accountant or bookkeeper right now?

| Yes, someone helps me | No, but I would like help | No, I do it all myself |

Great. We'll be with you every step of the way.

(Back)   **Next**

Choose the role that represents what you do in your business. Note that owner supersedes all other options, which include:

- **Owner**
- **Accountant**
- **Employer**
- **Bookkeeper**
- **It's something else** if none of the above apply to your situation.

Once you click on one of the above, you will then be asked if you have a bookkeeper or accountant right now:

Your options include:

- **Yes, someone helps me** indicating that you have a bookkeeper, accountant, or administrator that helps you with your accountant.
- **No, but I would like help** lets QBO send you a link to connect with accountants.
- **No, I do it all myself** means that you will be taking care of your own accounting.

Click on the situation that best applies to you. Then click **<Next>**.

3. The next step is to tell QBO what functions you intend to you use QBO for
    initially. Again, all of this can be changed later so select whatever you think
    is applicable at this stage.

3. What would you like to do in QuickBooks?

This is just to get you started. You can always do more later.

- **Send and track invoices** allows you to create and send Invoices to your
  Customers.
- **Organize your expenses** allows you to track and categorize Expenses.
- **Track your retail sales** applies to businesses that are in retail.
- **Track your sales tax** applies if you are registered for GST/HST and/or QST.
  If you are not registered, you can activate this if you do register in the
  future.

- **Pay your employees** allows you to subscribe to QBO's payroll module.
- **Track hours** lets you track time for your employees or subcontractors

Click on as many of the boxes that apply to your business at this time. Click on **<Next>** to go to the next step.

4. The final step asks you how you want to track income and Expenses, which in this context is asking you whether you want to link bank accounts. While I highly recommend using this feature, you should click **Manually add transactions** at this stage as we will go through the process of linking your bank and credit card accounts later in this book.

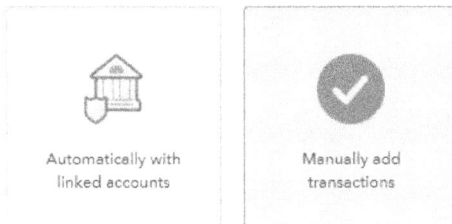

Click on **<All set>** which will take you to your QBO dashboard. You are now ready to get started!

BEST PRACTICES TO FOLLOW; COMMON MISTAKES TO AVOID

There are certain best practices to follow when starting your QBO file. This helps to prevent messy books and ensure that the data in your file is accurate; otherwise, financial reporting will be compromised or even meaningless. Also, if you have an accountant, it makes them happy and less likely to charge you additional fees.

- Set the correct year-end date as soon as you start your file. This is particularly applicable to corporations.

- Ensure that you choose the "accrual method" unless you specifically qualify as a business that is permitted to use the "cash method".

- Ensure that you have set up your Chart of Accounts properly and after giving it some thought. Also, have a process for setting up new accounts. If you have too many accounts, it can result in clutter on your Financial Statements while too few accounts do not allow for good insights and analysis.

- To avoid having too many accounts in your Chart of Accounts, make use of Products and Services. You can set up many different Products and Services that are all channeled into one income, Cost of Goods Sold, or Expense account on your Chart of Accounts.

- Use journal entries sparingly to enter unusual or one-off transactions. Most transactions can be entered through one of the other subledgers including Sales, Expenses, or Banking.

- QBO will often automatically assign transactions in the banking download to an uncategorized Expense or Asset. It is very easy to click **Add**; however, be mindful and take the few seconds to review the account category for each transaction to ensure that it isn't going to an uncategorized account.

- Ensure that you are using the correct tax code for each transaction. If you choose the wrong tax code, you will either understate or overstate your tax liability, which can result in penalties if audited, or a higher amount payable than is necessary.

- Get into the habit of reconciling your bank and credit card accounts every month as this will identify any potential errors or omissions early while you still remember the transactions.

- QBO allows you to enter transactions without a payee. It is easy, as you are zipping through the downloaded bank transactions, to forget to enter it. Note that it is always better to enter a payee, which takes a couple of extra seconds, as it allows for better reporting and can be very useful in case of audit.

- Review your Accounts Receivable and Accounts Payable Reports monthly to ensure there are no older outstanding balances that should be followed up on or written off.

- Make sure you don't duplicate transactions when adding them from the banking download.

- Have access to a resource that can help you review your QBO file, especially if you aren't sure about something. It is much easier to fix something early in the process than to go back and fix a host of problems.

- When creating Reports that you use frequently, click on **<Save customization>** to save the report in your **[Custom reports]**. This will save time and help you remember the reports that you have used in the past.

- Close your books at the end of your fiscal period to ensure that no changes are made to previous periods that have already been filed.

- Verify that the balance when filing your sales tax agrees to the Balance Sheet at the same date.

- Make use of the various time saving features of QBO, including entering transactions from the banking download, rules, receipts, recurring transactions, and copying transactions.

NAVIGATING QBO

Left-hand Navigation Bar

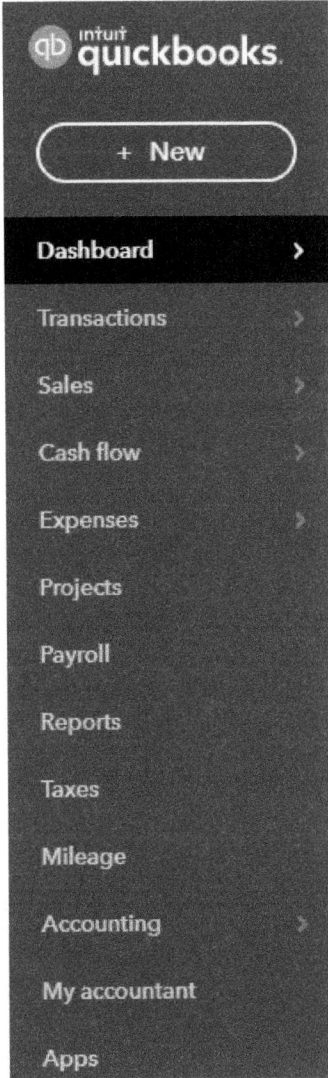

The **Left-hand Navigation Bar** is an important part of QBO's interface. It contains all of QBO's day-to-day functions, and it will always appear onscreen EXCEPT when you are entering transactions. We will briefly go through each of the tabs in order. Later in the book, we will explore most of these features in greater depth.

> ⚠ *Some versions of QBO use different terms for the items in the **Left-hand Navigation Bar**. These are indicated in parentheses where relevant.*
> *E.g., **Sales** > (or **Invoicing** >)*

+ New Button

There are various ways to enter transactions in QBO, which we will discuss as we go through each section. The options available by clicking on **< + New >** can be seen on the QBO interface as follows:

Clicking on **<+ New>** gives you a list of transactions that can be entered by simply clicking on the transaction type rather than going to the specific section. Almost every type of transaction is represented here. Using this method of entering transactions saves navigating through other menus.

Dashboard

The **Dashboard >** in QBO is a quick view of your business. There are two tabs, **[Get things done]** and **[Business overview]**.

Get things done Tab

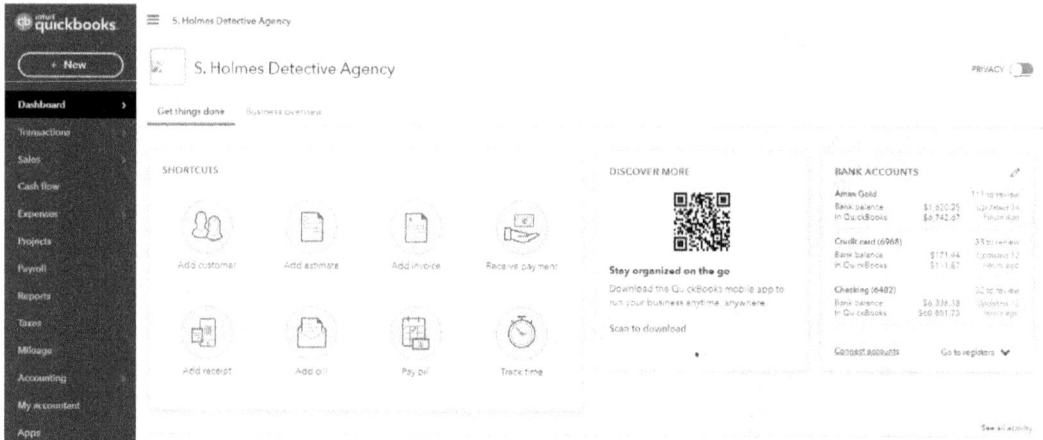

This tab shows you three sections. The first, **SHORTCUTS**, shows the most used functions in QBO including adding Customers, Estimates, Invoices, Bills, etc.

The next section entitled **DISCOVER MORE** gives you a QR code that you can scan to download the mobile app (or you can simply find the app in the Appstore connected to your phone). The mobile app has much of the functionality of the computer software and allows you to see your business, invoice customers, receive payments, etc., directly from the app.

The third section, **BANK ACCOUNTS**, lists your bank and credit card accounts and current balances, along with the option to **Connect accounts** or **Go to registers ▼** using a dropdown.

Business overview Tab

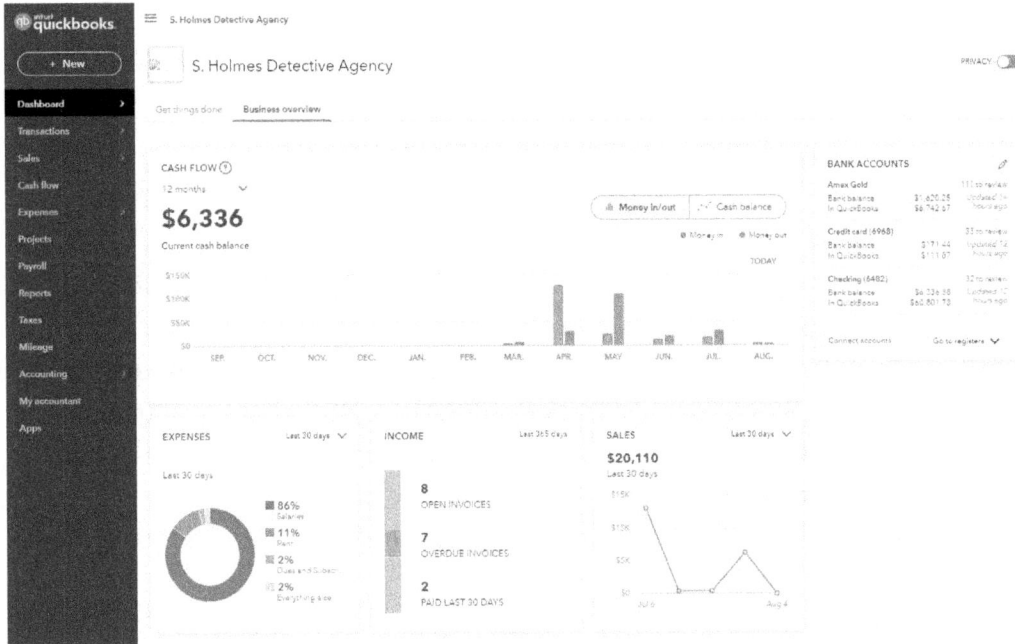

[**Business overview**] gives you a picture of your cash flow and charts for your Expenses, Sales, and Income. There is a limited amount of date customization for each chart that allows you to shorten or extend the period over which it is shown.

Transactions (or Banking)

The next section is **Transactions >** (some versions of QBO may display **Banking >** instead of **Transactions >**). All functions relating to banking are reflected here and are discussed in the section on linking bank accounts and entering banking transactions.

Sales (or Invoicing)

Sales > (or **Invoicing >** in some version of QBO) accesses all functions relating to sales and Customers and are discussed in the section on Create Customers and Invoices.

Cash Flow

This section shows you an overview of your cash flow and includes items that have been invoiced and not yet received as well as Bills and liabilities that have not yet been paid. This information is then extrapolated to show you your projected cash on hand.

Expenses

All functions relating to Suppliers, Bills, and Expenses can be accessed by clicking **Expenses >** and are discussed in the section on how to create Suppliers, Bills and Expenses.

Projects

Projects are useful for Customers where you generate multiple Invoices and/or have multiple Expenses that you want to track in one place. QBO allows you to assign each transaction to a specific project thereby allowing you to see all transactions that relate to the project on one interface and also to generate reports to assess the profitability and glean other insights into projects. This is an advanced topic that is beyond the scope of this book.

Payroll

QBO has an add-on that allows you to process payroll for your employees. I do not use QBO payroll as I have found other third-party payroll providers to provide a better service at a similar price point. Consequently, I will not be reviewing QBO payroll in this book.

Reports

QBO has numerous reports that are discussed in greater detail in the section on setting up and working with reports.

Taxes

Taxes refers to sales taxes, which are discussed in the sections on setting up sales tax and filing your sales tax return.

Mileage

A relatively new function, mileage allows you to track business travel. This is an advanced topic and beyond the scope of this book.

Accounting

The **Accounting >** section is where you will find your Chart of Accounts and Reconcile functions. These are discussed in the sections on setting up your chart of accounts and reconciling accounts.

My accountant

If you have one, you can set your accountant up in the Manage users section. Once set up, your accountant can submit requests for information and save documents that will then appear in this section.

Apps

QBO has a huge ecosystem of applications that work and integrate directly with QBO. There are apps to help you manage the sales process and Inventory, manage customer relationships, automatically retrieve bank statements, as well as advanced receipts apps that post transactions from a Bill or receipt directly to QBO, apps that help you import data from QBO into Excel, and many more. A more extensive discussion of QBO apps will be available in my next book.

Top Navigation Bar

- **☰Hamburger menu** allows you to hide the **Left-hand Navigation Bar**, giving you more room on your screen.

- **S. Holmes Detective Agency** is the name of our business. The name of your business will appear here. This is most useful if you have access to more than one company.

- **? Help** is QBO's resource section. Clicking on this will take you a list of resources where you can search for the issue you need help with.

- **⚲Search icon** allows you to search QBO by entering any search terms.

  Clicking on **⚲Search icon** brings up the following screen, which gives you some search tips and also the most recent transactions that have been entered.

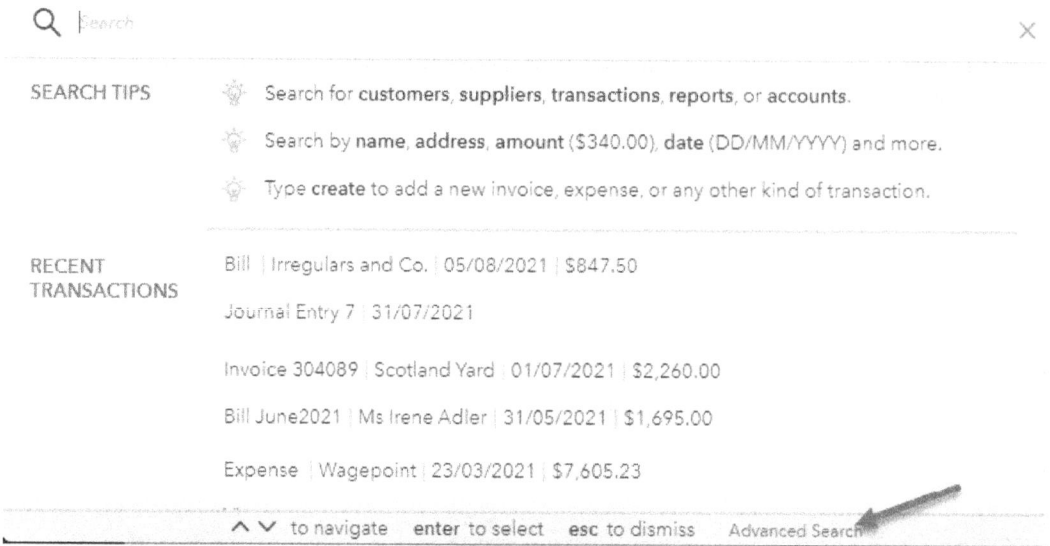

At the bottom of the Q **Search** window, you can click on **Advanced Search,** which will take you to an advanced search menu:

You can then enter a search query based on the type of transaction or various other fields which are included in the dropdown menus.

🔔 **Bell icon** is where you will see any notifications from QBO.

⚙️ **Gear icon** is where you will find all of the company settings, lists, and tools. We discuss this extensively in the following sections.

The "R" inside the circle is where you will see the first letter of the name that you used to sign up for QBO. Clicking it will open the area where you can manage your Intuit account. This is discussed in greater detail in marketing preferences.

Bottom Bar

Many windows and interface feature a **Bottom Bar** that contains buttons or commands specific to that interface. These are typically finishing commands, such as **<Save>** et cetera.

PART 2: QBO CUSTOMIZATION

⚙ **Gear icon** menu

CUSTOMIZE YOUR SETUP

This section comprehensively explores each of the options available to help you set up your QBO file. Almost everything relating to the set up of QBO can be found by clicking on the ⚙ **Gear icon** on the **Top Navigation Bar**, which will bring up the following screen:

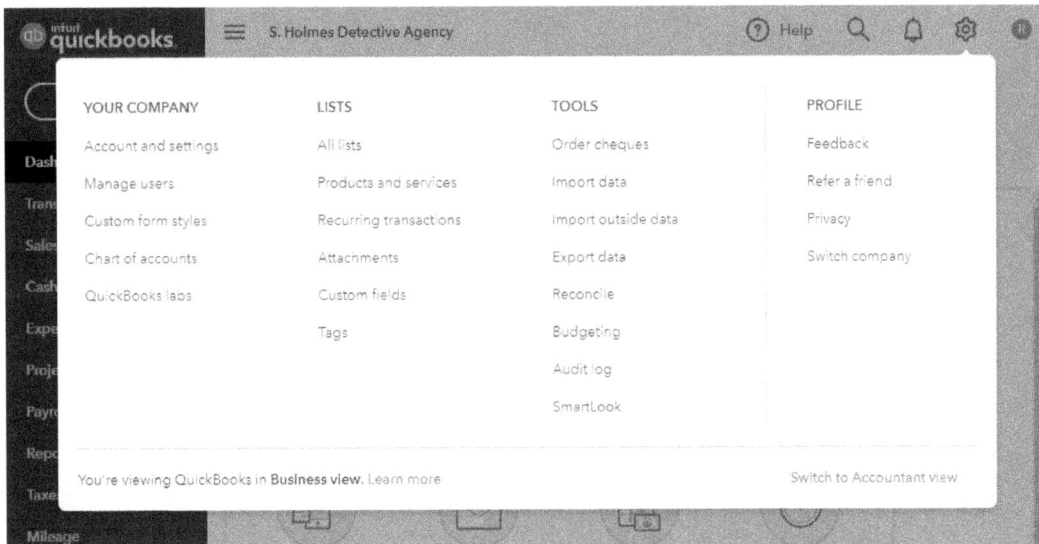

There are four columns: **YOUR COMPANY**, **LISTS**, **TOOLS**, and **PROFILE**. We will explore each of these columns, working down the lists of features.

YOUR COMPANY

This section is where you customize details relating to your business and configure the features that you will use on a day-to-day basis. It is important to familiarize yourself with each of these sections.

Account and settings

Click on the ⚙ **Gear icon** and then **Account and settings** under **YOUR COMPANY**. That will bring up the following interface, where we will begin setting up your QBO file:

You will see several tabs on the left-hand side. Each tab allows for customization of the various features that are available in QBO. To select a tab, click it. While you might not need every feature when starting your business, it is important to know what types of features are available. We will now go through each tab, beginning with **[Company]**, which is the default.

Company Tab

This is where you set up details relating to your company. To edit a section, click the ✏️**Pencil Icon**.

Account and Settings   Help   ✕

Company	Company name		
Billing & Subscription			
Sales			
Expenses		Company name	S.Holmes Detective Agency
		Legal name	Same as company name
Payments		Business Number (BN)	123456789
Advanced	Company type	Tax form	.
		Industry	.
	Contact info	Company email	watson@shda.com
		Customer-facing email	Same as company email
		Company phone	.
		Website	.
	Address	Company address	, ON
	Address	Customer-facing address	Same as company address
	Address	Legal address	Same as company address
	Communications with Intuit	Marketing Preferences	

⚙ **Gear icon** menu → **YOUR COMPANY: Account and settings**

Company name

- **Company logo** will let you set up your logo by importing an image file from your computer. You can also leave this blank and set it up later. Note that the image that you import should have square dimensions.
- **Company name** is where you enter the operating name of your business.
- **Legal name** of your business may be different from your operating name, and you can also enter it here. For example, you might officially have a numbered company that you refer to by its operating or another informal name.
- **Business Number (BN)** is the one issued to you by Revenue Canada if you are a corporation. If you are a registered sole proprietorship, you would use the number issued by a provincial authority, e.g., the NEQ issued by Revenue Quebec. If you have not registered your sole proprietorship, you can leave this blank.

Once you have completed setting this up, click on **<Save>**. Otherwise, your changes will not be recorded.

Company type

- **Tax form ▾** allows you to enter the legal structure of your business. Choose one of the options from the dropdown that most closely applies to your business.
- **Industry** refers to your business's sector category. When you start to enter your industry, several options show up that can be selected that mostly accurately apply to your business. If none of these options are appropriate, you can select General Product or General Service-based Business. You can also leave this blank.

Click on **<Save>**.

Contact info

There are options that allow you to have a different email and address for the business and another one that is shown to the customer.

Enter your:

- Company email
- Customer-facing email
- Company phone
- Website

Note that these are all optional fields. The information entered here will show up on your invoice, which we will discuss in greater detail later.

Once updated, click on **<Save>**.

Address

There are three different **Address** sections:

- **Company address**
- **Customer-facing address** if different from the company address.
- **Legal address** if different from the company address.

Once updated, click on **<Save>**.

Communications with Intuit

The final option in **[Company]** is a link to **Marketing Preferences** where you control how QBO communicates with you.

Clicking on it will take you the screen below. You can also review your **Sign in & security**, **Personal info**, **Data privacy**, and **Products & billing**.

≡ intuit ®

R

Hello Ronika!

Here's where you can manage the details of your Intuit Account.

Sign in & security

Update the way you sign in to your Intuit products.

Manage sign in & security

Personal info

Change the info we use to personalize your products.

Manage personal info

Data privacy

Stay in control of your data and how it's used.

Manage data privacy

Products & billing

See all your products in one place and manage your subscriptions.

Manage products & billing

⚙ **Gear icon** menu → **YOUR COMPANY: Account and settings**

Billing & Subscription Tab

The next tab, **[Billing & Subscription]**, shows you details about your QBO subscription:

Account and Settings

Company	Company ID
Billing & Subscription	Payment Method **VISA** Visa ▪▪▪▪ (expires 11/2023) ✏
Sales	Allow billing transfer to your accountant?
Expenses	
Payments	
Advanced	

QuickBooks Plus

SUBSCRIBED Next charge on 04-08-2021

$60/mo

+ applicable taxes

Downgrade your plan

View payment history

Cancel subscription

Switch to annual billing

QuickBooks Payroll

CANCELLED ON 04-05-2017

You have access to data and reporting until one year. You can Resubscribe to pick up where you left off if you decide to come back

(Resubscribe)

QuickBooks Time

Track time on any device to streamline payroll, send accurate invoices, and save thousands each year.

- Let employees clock in and out from their devices
- Build, edit, and share schedules by jobs or shifts
- Automatically add employee timesheets for faster, more accurate time entry

- **Company ID i**s a number automatically assigned by QBO.
- **Payment Method** is the credit card info attached to your QBO account. If you would like to change the credit card or update the expiry date, it can be done by clicking on the ✏ **Pencil Icon**.

- **Allow billing transfer to your accountant**? Can be beneficial to some as QBO Pro-Advisors get a reduced rate which they might pass along. Alternatively, many accountants will include the cost of the QBO subscription with their accounting fees, which are often billed monthly.

The boxes provide details about your current billing plan, which in our example is QBO Plus. There are also options to **Downgrade** or **Upgrade your plan**, **View payment history**, and **Cancel subscription**. You can also **Switch to annual billing**, which can result in some savings but removes the option to cancel your plan at any time.

If you wish to subscribe to QuickBooks Payroll and QuickBooks Time, you may do so from here as well.

Sales Tab

There is a significant amount of customization available for sales forms (Invoices and Estimates). You can format what types of fields appear on the sales forms and customize the type of information that is reflected on your product and/or service descriptions (which will be discussed in greater detail in the create Customers and Invoices section). As with most customization, you don't have to select everything you need at this stage. Just be aware that the option is available and, if the need arises, you can come back to this section and change or turn on the customization. To edit a section, click the ✏ **Pencil Icon**.

> ➤ *The screenshot below shows all the available options in the Plus version of QBO. Options not available in Essentials and EasyStart will be noted.*

⚙ **Gear icon** menu → **YOUR COMPANY: Account and settings**

Account and Settings   ⑦ Help ✕

Company	Customize	Customize the way forms look to your customers		**[1]** Customize look and feel
Billing & Subscription				
Sales	Sales form content	Preferred invoice terms		✎
		Preferred delivery method	Print later	
Expenses		Shipping	On	
		Custom fields		
Payments		Custom transaction numbers	On	**[2]**
		Service date	On	
Advanced		Discount	On	
		Deposit	On	
		Tags	On	
	Products and services	Show Product/Service column on sales forms	On	✎
		Show SKU column	Off	
		Turn on price rules	Off	**[3]**
		Track quantity and price/rate	On	
		Track inventory quantity on hand	On	
	Progress invoicing	Create multiple partial invoices from a single estimate	On	**[4]** ✎
	Messages	Default email message sent with sales forms		**[5]** ✎
	Reminders	Default email message for invoice reminders		**[6]** ✎
		Automatic invoice reminders	Off	
	Online delivery	Email options for all sales forms		**[7]** ✎
	Statements	Show aging table at bottom of statement	On	**[8]** ✎

Done

1. Customize

Click **<Customize look and feel>** to set up the format of Invoices to be sent to Customers. You can create one from scratch or you can import an Invoice style using a Microsoft Word file. If you do decide to import a style, note that there are fairly specific formatting rules. Essentially, the Word document must contain tables with the headings you want to appear on your invoice. You can also import colours and fonts. QBO provides a style guide as well as some templates that allow you to format an existing invoice style or one that you have created.

If you create a new invoice style, QBO gives you a default where you can choose your colours and provides a limited selection of fonts and templates. You can also change the placement of the content and decide what fields to show on the Invoice.

A more comprehensive review of customizing your Invoices and Estimates can be found in the custom forms style section.

> ⚠ *Invoices to Canadian Customers must contain your business GST and QST numbers, if applicable. This setting can be updated when you set up your sales taxes.*

2. Sales Form Content

There are several customization options in this section.

- **Preferred invoice terms** refers to the amount of time a customer has to pay an Invoice after it has been sent. This can be anywhere from immediately, also referred to as due on receipt, to a fixed number of days that can be customized. QBO might give you some options to start or you can simply set them up manually. There is no limit to how many invoice terms you can add.

You can set up an Invoice term for either a fixed number of days or you can make invoices payable on a certain day of the month.

The term automatically calculates a due date on the Invoice and reflects it as a separate field so that the customer will see the date payable when they receive the Invoice.

Setting up terms is discussed in greater detail in the terms section.

- **Preferred delivery method** allows you to choose whether you would like to have a default setting for your invoice to print later or send later via email. If you don't want to set a default you can simply leave it blank.
- **Shipping** when toggled on will show a shipping field on your invoice. If you sell products and charge shipping to your Customers, you can click on the box to turn it on. Otherwise, you can leave it off.

> ✓ *An alternative to toggling the shipping field on is to create a "shipping" item which we will discuss in the Products and Services section.*

- **Custom fields** (Essentials and Plus only) allows you to create up to 3 additional fields that you might want to track separately on your Invoices.

The most popular example of a custom field is for sales reps, which is not currently available as a separate field in QBO. If you would like to track the performance of your sales reps, you would create a custom field in this section. Other types of custom fields might be customer types, purchase order numbers and other info that is specific to your industry. Once you have created custom fields, you can generate reports that allow you to further drill down into your data.

- **Custom transaction numbers** when turned on, allows you to enter custom invoice numbers. If you leave this off, QBO will automatically assign the next transaction number based on a sequence using the previous transaction number.

- **Service date** is useful for tradespeople or other service-based businesses where the date on which a service is provided is different from the date of the Invoice. Alternatively, you might have several dates on which you provided the service, but only bill once a month or periodically. Turning this on creates a field where you can enter the service date on an Invoice.

- **Discount** creates a box for discounts on the Invoice under the sub-total. You can then select a discount amount or a percentage directly under the subtotal field and QBO will automatically calculate it and deduct it from the Invoice.

✓ *Similar to shipping, instead of toggling the discount field, you can create an a "discount" item which is discussed in the Products and Services section.*

Below is a screenshot of an Invoice with all of the above options toggled on.

> ➢ *All of the options discussed above, except for **Custom Fields**, are available in all versions of QBO.*

🕙 **Invoice no.304090**   ⚙ ⓘ Help ✕

Customer ⓘ	Customer email ⓘ	Cc/Bcc	Get set up ☐ Cards VISA		BALANCE DUE
[field] ∨	[field]				**$0.00**
	☐ Send later ⓘ				

Billing address	Terms ⓘ	Invoice date	Due date		Invoice no.
	▼	26/08/2021	26/08/2021		304090
		Create recurring invoice			
	Sales Reps				Location
					Ontario ▼
	Not printed on form				

Tags ⓘ   Manage tags
[Start typing to add a tag]

Amounts are   Exclusive of Tax ▼

#	SERVICE DATE	PRODUCT/SERVICE ⓘ	DESCRIPTION	QTY	RATE	AMOUNT	SALES TAX	CLASS	
⊞	1								🗑
⊞	2								🗑

[Add lines] [Clear all lines] [Add subtotal]   Subtotal $0.00

Message on invoice   Discount percent ▼ [   ] $0.00
[Thank you for your business]

                                                                         Total $0.00

                                                                         Deposit

Message on statement   Balance due $0.00
[field]

[Cancel]   Print or Preview | Make recurring | Customize   [Save] [Save and send ▼]

> ✓ *You should only turn on the fields that you need to avoid blank or unused boxes on your invoice and so that it looks professional, since it is seen by your Customers.*

3. Products and services

A product and service, also referred to as an item, is a separate type of categorization in QBO.

The primary type of categorization in any accounting system is the Chart of Accounts as explained in the Chart of Accounts section. Each account in the Chart of Accounts shows up as a line item on your Financial Statements.

If you provide several types of Products and Services, you could create a separate account for each on your Chart of Accounts. This would however create clutter by adding too much detail to your Financial Statements.

To avoid this issue, QBO allows for the creation of unlimited Products and Services that are summarized to the specific account category, in the Chart of Accounts, that you select for the product or service.

> ❖ *For example, SHDA provides several sizes and types of magnifying glass. On their Chart of Accounts, they have one account called "sales of products". They want to be able to create a more detailed description on their Invoices, track Inventory of the various sizes, and create reports to see exactly how many magnifying glasses they have sold by type and size. Consequently, they create several "product" types for each size and type of magnifier, all of which are then further categorized to the sale of products account on the chart of accounts. This allows them to see reports by each type of magnifying glass, while only seeing one sales of product account on their Profit and Loss Statement.*

- **Show Product/Service column on sales forms** allows you to show a field for the product or service that you are providing. Additionally, by toggling this feature on, you may create as many Products and Services as you require for which you can then create reports to analyze the performance of each product and/or service.
- **Show SKU Column** adds a field for SKUs which is useful if you sell products for which you use SKUs.
- **Turn on price rules** (Plus) is a relatively new feature in QBO that allows you to charge different prices to different Customers for the same product or services. Toggle this on if you would like to use this feature.
- **Track quantity and price/rate** allows you to enter the quantity of a product or service and the individual rates for each unit. This is especially useful if you are selling more than one of a specific product or for service-based businesses that charge by the hour.
- **Track Inventory quantity on hand** (Plus) allows you to track the amount of Inventory products that you have on hand. This is useful to see what is available in Inventory and allows you to make more effective re-ordering decisions. If you sell products and are using the Inventory module in QBO, you must turn this on to effectively track Inventory amounts.

For additional details, refer to the section on setting up Products and Services.

4. Progress Invoicing

Progress invoicing is a QBO feature that lets you split an estimate into as many Invoices as are required based on the invoicing schedule that you have with your customer. After you create an estimate, you can then invoice Customers for partial payments as you complete the work. You can also add new items as your work progresses from the initial estimate to Progress Invoices.

5. Messages

QBO allows you to email your Invoices and Estimates. This option allows you to create and customize a default message that accompanies the actual invoice or estimate. Additionally, you can choose to CC or BCC specific email addresses. A standard message is already entered, which you can then customize or leave as is.

Account and Settings

Company		
	Messages	Default email message sent with sales forms
Billing & Subscription		☑ Use greeting Dear ▼ [Full Name] ▼
		Sales form ⑦
Sales		Invoice ▼ **Use standard message**
Expenses		Email subject line
		Invoice [Invoice No.] from S. Holmes D
Payments		Email message
Advanced		We appreciate your business. Please find your invoice details here. Feel free to contact us if you have any questions. Have a great day!
		Have a great day, S. Holmes Detective Agency
		☐ Email me a copy at watson@shda.com
		Copy (Cc) new invoices to address
		Cc (Separate multiple emails with a comma)
		Blind Copy (Bcc) new invoices to address
		Bcc (Separate multiple emails with a comma)
		Sales form
		Estimate ▼ ⑦

Cancel   **Save**

6. Reminders

When Invoices are overdue, QBO allows you to send pre-formatted reminders. These can be done manually through **Sales >** (or **Invoicing >**) in the **Left-hand Navigation Bar** (see below) or you can set up rules for overdue Invoices that are then sent automatically along with a default message. You have the option to set up a series of up to 3 reminders for which you can establish the dates relative to the invoice date.

7. Online Delivery

All Invoices can be emailed to Customers and clients. The online delivery option allows you to customize what your Customers will see, which is either a short summary or the full details of the Invoice in the email that you send to them. You can also choose whether to attach the PDF of the Invoice and whether the formatting is plain text.

8. Statements

If you have Customers who have more than one invoice overdue or who want details about their Invoices and payments, you can send them statements. This option in settings allows you to customize the statement by showing them in a summary or detail format.

The aging table at the bottom of the statement breaks up the amounts payable in 30-day increments, which can be useful if your Customers have terms such as Net 30 or Net 60 which shows them the exact amount that is overdue.

Expenses Tab (Essentials and Plus)

Bills are Invoices received from Suppliers or vendors that will be paid at a later date. From an accounting standpoint, this is a two-step process—when a Bill is entered in QBO, it is recorded as an Accounts Payable. Once payment is made it is removed from Accounts Payable and the payment is deducted from the bank account. Bill payments are only available in the Essentials and Plus version, since not all businesses require this functionality.

An Expense in QBO terminology is also a payment to a supplier, similar to a Bill, except that you are effectively entering the Bill and paying it at the same time. Instead of adding it to Accounts Payable, the bank account is deducted directly. This means that you do not have the ability to review the balances that you owe to

Suppliers and pay them at a later date through QBO, which can be useful to track how much you owe at any given time and make cash flow decisions.

Often, small service-based businesses have a minimal number of payments owing to Suppliers. As such, tracking how much you owe is not necessary, and you can simply record the Expense when you pay it.

Below is the screen for **[Expenses]**. To edit a section, click the ✏ **Pencil Icon**:

Account and Settings

Company	Bills and expenses	Show Items table on expense and purchase forms	On	1	✏
Billing & Subscription		Show Tags field on expense and purchase forms	On		
		Track expenses and items by customer	On		
Sales		Make expenses and items billable	On		
Expenses		Default bill payment terms			
Payments	Purchase orders	Use purchase orders	On	2	✏
Advanced	Messages	Default email message sent with purchase orders		3	✏

Done

1. **Bills and expenses**

   - **Show Items table on expense and purchase forms** allows you to enter Expenses either by using Categories, which is the default, or by using items which are created in the Products or services section. Items can be the same as the ones you have created for your sales form content, or you can create specific items for Expenses.

❖ *For example, SHDA would like to track the lenses and handles that they buy from their supplier, Magnussen Electronics. There are often several different types of these items on each Bill. Rather than using Expense categories (from the Chart of Accounts) SHDA selects items which allows them to create and enter each individual item from the Bill. All items would then be categorized to one purchases account which is a sub-account of Cost of Goods Sold. This allows them to track and report on the items purchased and ensure that their Inventory quantities are up to date.*

⚙ **Gear icon** menu → **YOUR COMPANY: Account and settings**

- **Show Tags field on expense and purchase forms** is a customizable label that
  allows you to create reports for that label, thereby allowing for deeper
  analysis into your business.

❖ *For example, SHDA would like to track consulting services to clients with dogs.
Rather than create a separate service item for this purpose, they can simply
create a tag called "clients with dogs" that will allow them to generate a report
that tracks sales and Expenses for "clients with dogs". You can turn on this
feature in this section so that a "tag" field is available on your Bills and
Expenses.*

- **Track expenses and items by customer** creates a "customer" field in your
  Bills and Expenses where you can assign Expenses incurred to specific
  Customers. This allows you to create reports which track Expenses by
  customer.
- **Make expenses and items billable** lets you indicate that specific expenses
  are billable to your customer. By activating this field, QBO allows you to
  check a box on the Bill or Expense indicating that it is billable. Then, when
  creating an Invoice for a customer, you will be able to see a dropdown of
  billable Expenses that can be directly added to the Invoice rather than re-
  entering the information manually.
- **Default bill payment terms**, similar to Invoices, represent payment terms
  such as due within 30 days or upon receipt. If you have a term that occurs
  more frequently than others, you can enter it here as a default, saving some
  time on data entry.

2. Purchase orders (POs)

Product-based business often use purchase orders (POs) to order goods from
Suppliers. A P.O. will have most of the information that is found on a Bill on which

information relating to the purchase such as the supplier, quantity, rate, date description etc. are entered and sent to the supplier. When the supplier fulfills the purchase order, it can be converted to a Bill directly without having to create a new Bill. Additionally, you can add up to 3 **Custom fields** if there is specific info that you would like to see and a field for it does not exist. An example of this would be the sales order number provided by the supplier.

Custom transaction numbers can be entered on a PO, or you can let QBO automatically assign the numbers in sequential order.

Default message on purchase orders can be customized in this section, which will then be reflected in the body on all purchase orders. These can also be entered directly onto the purchase order.

3. Messages

You can include a default email message when you send a purchase order to your supplier. To see how messages work, please refer to our section on Messages in the Sales Tab.

Payments Tab

QBO is also a payment processor. If you invoice Customers/clients and would like to accept credit cards using QBO, you can apply for an account directly through this tab.

Account and Settings

Company	QuickBooks Payments	Get paid more ways, fast!
Sales		• Accept credit card payments through QuickBooks and emailed invoices
		• Accept payments through QuickBooks, emailed invoices, and mobile
Expenses		• Clear and simple pricing
Payments		

Learn more

The current fees per transaction are $0.25 and 2.95% of the amount of the sale. E.g., a $1,000.00 sale will cost $0.25+ $29.50 = $29.75 in merchant processing fees.

Click **<Learn more>** to begin the process. After you have submitted your application, it will likely take a few days to process your info. QBO will either approve your application or ask for additional info.

⚙️ **Gear icon** menu → **YOUR COMPANY: Account and settings**

Once you have been approved for payments, the following fields will appear when you click **[Payments]**:

Settings

Company	Merchant details	Merchant ID	
Notifications		For other changes to your Payments account, please call us. (855) 253-1536	
Sales			
	Deposit accounts	Standard deposits	Change
Expenses			
Payments			
	Documents	Monthly Statements	Select a mo... ⌄ View
Advanced			
	Chart of Accounts	Tell us where in QuickBooks to automatically record:	
		Standard deposits	TD Bank
		Processing fees	QuickBooks Payments Fees
	Payment Methods	Cards ⎯⎯, 💳 VISA Pay	

- **Merchant details** is your QBO issued payment ID and a phone number in case of issues.
- **Deposit accounts** lists the bank account for your business. This can be modified using **Change**.
- **Documents** includes the monthly credit card statements for each month that you can download and save in your accounting folder.
- **Chart of accounts** is where you indicate the account category to which the credit card payments and related fees should be allocated. Once set up, the payments will be automatically allocated to these accounts.
- **Standard deposits** is usually the business bank account where the payments are deposited, or they can be an undeposited funds account. If you are using an undeposited funds account, make sure that you reconcile these to your bank account on a regular basis otherwise you will have duplicate payments and reconciliation issues.
- **Processing fees** is the account where the charges relating to the credit card payments are shown. You can either create a separate account called "QuickBooks payments fees" or, if you only process a few charges per year, you can allocate them to a "bank charges" account to which all bank related fees are allocated. To create a new account, please refer to the Create a New Account in Chart of Accounts section.

- **Payment Methods** shows icons for the various credit cards that QBO accepts.

> ➤ *American Express is currently accepted.*

⚙ **Gear icon** menu → **YOUR COMPANY: Account and settings**

Advanced Tab

Here you will find a variety of advanced accounting settings. To edit a section, click the ✎ **Pencil Icon**:

Account and Settings   I Help ✕

Company	Accounting	First month of fiscal year	December	✎
Billing & Subscription		First month of income tax year	Same as fiscal year	
		Accounting method	**1** Accrual	
Sales		Close the books	Off	
		Default tax rate selection	Exclusive of Tax	
Expenses				
Payments	Company type	Tax form	**2** Corporation, one or more shareholders	✎
Advanced	Chart of accounts	Enable account numbers	Off	✎
		Shipping account	Shipping Income	
		Discount account	**3** Discounts given	
		Billable expense income account	Billable Expense Incor	
	Categories	Track classes	**4** On	✎
		Track locations	On	
	Automation	Pre-fill forms with previously entered content	Off	✎
		Automatically apply credits	Off	
		Automatically invoice unbilled activity	**5** Off	
		Automatically apply bill payments	Off	
	Projects	Organize all job-related activity in one place	**6** On	✎
	Time tracking	Add Service field to timesheets	On	✎
		Make Single-Time Activity Billable to Customer	**7** On	
	Language	Language	**8** English	✎
	Currency	Home Currency	Canadian Dollar	✎
		Multicurrency	**9** Off	
	Other preferences	Date format	**10** dd/MM/yyyy	✎
		Number format	123,456.00	
		Warn if duplicate cheque number is used	On	
		Warn me when I enter a bill number that's already been used for that supplier	Off	
		Warn if duplicate journal number is used	Off	
		Sign me out if inactive for	1 hour	

⚙ **Gear icon** menu → **YOUR COMPANY: Account and settings**

1. **Accounting**

   - **First month of the fiscal year end** for a sole proprietorship will almost
     always be January 1st.

     As a corporation, the first month of your fiscal year will depend on your year
     end date. This can be found by looking at your business's year end Financial
     Statements or corporate tax return. If this is your first year in business, then
     you have to determine the year end that was established at the time of
     incorporation. If no year end was set up, my advice is usually to choose the
     end of the month of the following year preceding the date of the
     incorporation.

   ❖ *For example, if your corporation was set up on May 15th, you can set your year*
   end at April 30th. Note that once selected, all future tax filings will reflect this as
   your year end date. A final option is to keep it simple and choose December
   31st.

   - **First month of income tax year** is usually the same as the first month of your
     fiscal year per above. In the rare case where this is different, you would use
     this to set up a different year end.
   - **Accounting method** choices are either **Accrual** or **Cash**. Most businesses use
     the accrual method, which is required by Revenue Canada for almost all
     businesses. The only businesses that Revenue Canada allows to use the cash
     method are farmers, fishers, or self-employed commissioned sales agents.

   ➢ *Accrual Method vs Cash Method of Accounting*

   ⇨ *After selling a product or providing a service, many businesses invoice their*
   Customers and allow them to pay after some time has elapsed (see invoice
   terms). Similarly, you will receive Bills from your Suppliers/vendors that
   allow you to pay the amount due on a specified due date that is after the
   date of the Bill. Accounting systems that use the accrual method will record
   the Invoice or Bill on the date it is issued regardless of payment date (there
   are exceptions for when the full product or service is delivered over time such
   as you would see in construction or setting up an IT system). This then flows
   through to the Profit and Loss Statement on the date of the Invoice/bill which
   is what taxes payable are based upon.

> ⇨ *Businesses that use the cash method only reflect the transaction as a sale or Expense on the Profit and Loss Statement when the Invoice or Bill has been paid rather than the date on which the product or service is provided. This method is usually appropriate when payment is uncertain.*

- **Close the books** allows you to designate a date before which no changes can be made without a warning or a warning/password combination. The purpose of this function is to ensure that transactions are not changed once your year end has been finalized and Financial Statements and tax returns have been prepared and submitted.
- **Default tax rate selection** lets you choose a default tax type. There are three options available here:
- **Exclusive of tax** means you would enter an Invoice/bill before sales tax. QBO will then calculate the taxes on top of the invoice amount to arrive at a final amount including taxes. This is useful when you invoice Customers a net amount and add taxes on top of it based on the appropriate tax rate.
- **Inclusive of tax** means that you would enter the total amount of the Invoice including sales tax. QBO then calculates the sales tax and net amount based on the total amount. If you use **Inclusive of tax**, you should verify that the taxes calculated by QBO agree to the amount on the Invoice or Bill.
- **Out of scope tax** means that taxes are simply not applicable to a transaction. This is used when you are either not registered for sales tax or in the case of non-taxable transactions such as transfers between accounts or personal purchases that are allocated to the shareholder loan account.

2. Company Type

- **Tax form ▼** is a dropdown for the business structure that represents your business. This is used by QBO in conjunction with the tax products that they offer and doesn't impact any other aspects of your file.

3. Chart of accounts

Setting up a Chart of Accounts is discussed in the Chart of Accounts chapter.

- **Enable account numbers** allows you to have numbers in addition to names. Very small businesses do not usually require numbers. This becomes more important as your business grows and becomes more complex. There are conventions used by accountants when numbering your Chart of Accounts.
- **Shipping account** (Essentials and Plus) is the account that corresponds to shipping on sales form content, when activated. You can simply create a new shipping income account, or you can combine it with another account.
- **Discount account** (Essentials and Plus) similarly corresponds to the discount from the sales form content.
- **Billable expense** (Essentials and Plus) income account corresponds to the billable Expenses discussed in the Bills and Expenses section.

4. Categories (Plus)

This is a powerful feature of QBO that allows you to toggle class or location fields or both. This is an advanced topic beyond the scope of this book.

5. Automation

Different levels of automation are available to activate in this section.

> ⚠ *This feature can help save time but can also be problematic if used improperly.*

- **Pre-fill forms with previously entered content** allows QBO to enter the details from the last transaction of the same type for the same customer, supplier, or employee. This can be useful if transactions are similar for each type of supplier or customer but otherwise it is better to leave this off as you can inadvertently overwrite a transaction.
- **Automatically apply credits** is a feature that applies any outstanding credits for a customer to the next invoice created for that same customer, automatically. This is useful when credits are being used sequentially; however, this should be turned off if credits are applied specifically to Invoices and not just to the next invoice for that customer.

- **Automatically invoice unbilled activity** (`Essentials` and `Plus`) creates Invoices for Customers who have Bills that have not yet been converted into Invoices.
- **Automatically apply bill payments** (`Essentials` and `Plus`) to the oldest Bill for the same supplier. Turning this on can make Bill paying easier—unless you don't pay your Bills chronologically but using some other method.

> ➢ *All automation functions above can be edited and unapplied, which is useful on an exceptional basis. However, if you find yourself unapplying them regularly, then it might be better to just turn off the automation.*

6. Projects (`Plus`)

When you have a business that regularly works on projects such as web development or construction, projects can be a useful tool to track all your income and Expenses in one place. You can also add old transactions to new projects by selecting the project name in the transaction window for Invoices, Bills, and Expenses, or create them directly through **[Projects]**. Once set up, you can run project-specific reports from a single dashboard. This is an advanced topic beyond the scope of this book.

7. Time tracking (`Essentials` and `Plus`)

Time tracking allows you to track time for your employees and subcontractors. This is an advanced topic and beyond the scope of this book.

8. Language

You can choose English or French as your language of choice for QBO Canada.

9. Currency (`Essentials` and `Plus`)

QBO allows for you to set up different currencies for transactions. This is only advisable if you have more than a few transactions a year in foreign currencies such as Invoices to Customers or Suppliers located in other countries whom you pay in a foreign currency. If you use a Canadian dollar (CAD) credit card for which you occasionally have non-CAD transactions, then there is no need to use foreign currency since the conversion is performed by the credit card issuer and not through your accounting software. Once activated, foreign currency cannot be deactivated, and since there is an additional layer of complexity with foreign currencies it is only advisable to activate this feature if necessary.

- **Home Currency** is where you set your reporting currency. Most businesses in Canada would use CAD unless their year end financial and tax reporting is in another currency. This might be applicable to corporations that have specifically elected to report in USD with Revenue Canada or for companies or divisions located outside Canada.
- **Multicurrency** is where you decide whether you are going to activate multicurrency. QBO advises you of the implications:

Currency   Home Currency   CAD - Canadian Dollar ▼

Multicurrency ⑦   ●○

Multicurrency may be right for you if you have financial
transactions in more than one currency.
Need help deciding about multicurrency?

Once you turn on Multicurrency:
- You can't turn it off
- You can't change your home currency
- Extra fields, columns and more are added to
  QuickBooks
- Some features may no longer be available

☐ I understand I can't undo Multicurrency

(Cancel) (Save)

You cannot turn **Multicurrency** off, which means that, once activated, you cannot revert back to a single currency if in the future you decide you no longer need multicurrency. This does not mean that your file becomes unusable, just that you will have all the extra features that come with multicurrency.

> ⚠ *You can't change your home currency from what was originally selected when multicurrency is turned on.*

10. Other preferences

- **Date format** is your preferred format. Some have a preference for the US system, which is month/day/year, while others might simply select day/month/year.
- **Number format** usually uses commas to denote thousands; however, some might prefer periods if they are accustomed to the French system.

⚙️ **Gear icon** menu → **YOUR COMPANY: Account and settings**

- **Warn if duplicate cheque number is used** will help you to avoid duplicate cheque numbers if you use cheques to pay Suppliers or employees.
- **Warn me when I enter a bill number that's already been used for that supplier** is a useful feature that helps to avoid entering a Bill that has already been entered.
- Warn if duplicate journal number is used applies to journal entries.
- **Sign me out if inactive for**▼ brings up a dropdown that lets you select a length of time of time after which QBO will sign you out for security purposes.

Manage users

When you sign up for QBO, you are automatically entered as the primary admin on the account.

You might, however, want to give access to additional users. This could include:

- A bookkeeper, so that they can enter transactions and prepare reports.
- An accountant to review transactions, make adjustments and review reports.
- An internal employee who may only be responsible for handling some part of your accounting.
- A contractor or employee who you would like to enter their time for time tracking purposes.

User limits for each version of QBO are listed below:

User Limits in QuickBooks Online

Note: Only administrators and standard users count toward your billable user limit.

EasyStart	1 billable user + 2 accounting firms
Essentials	3 billable users + 2 accounting firms
Plus	5 billable users + 2 accounting firms

⚙️ Gear icon menu → **YOUR COMPANY: Manage users**

To add a user, go to the ⚙️ **Gear icon** interface, and select **Manage Users** under **YOUR COMPANY**.

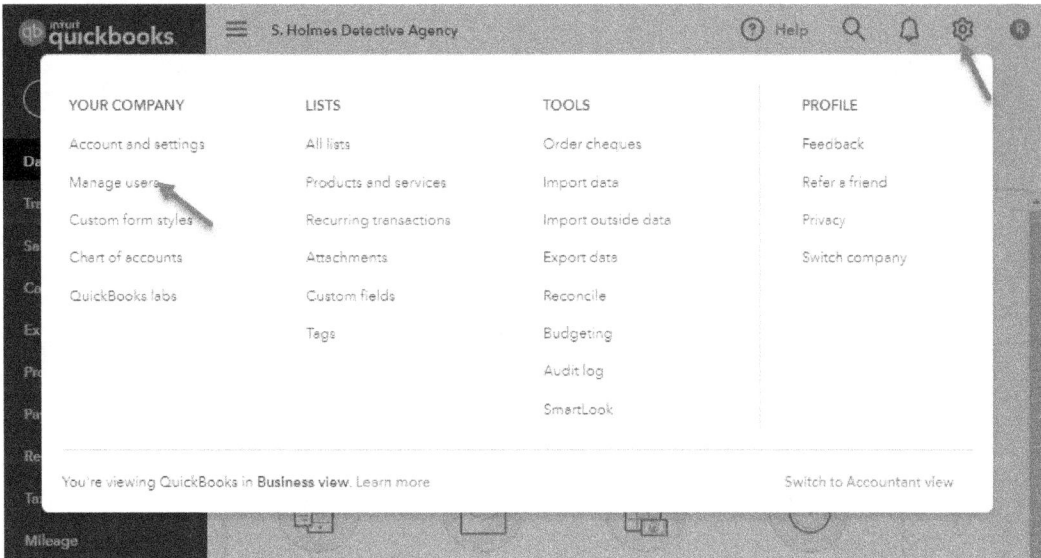

Users Tab

From **[Users]**, Click on **<Add User>**.

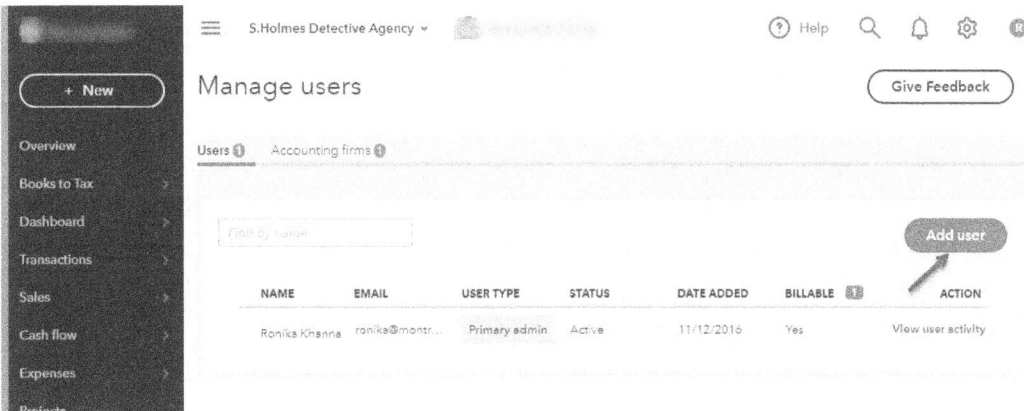

A new window will open.

There are several levels of users that you can add:

Add a new user   ✕
_____

Select user type

These count toward your user limit.

⦿ Standard user

   You can give them full or limited access, without admin privileges.

◯ Company admin

   They can see and do everything. This includes sending money, changing passwords, and
   adding users. Not everyone should be an admin.

These don't count toward your user limit.

◯ Reports only

   They can see all reports, except ones that show payroll or contact info.

◯ Time tracking only

   They can add their own time sheets.

                                                                        [Next]

- **Standard User** allows you to customize the access level to QBO.
- **Company admin** gives access to all functionality in QBO. You can have more than one company admin.
- **Reports only** allows the user to access reports only and doesn't count towards your user limit. This is useful when you are responsible for accounting in the company and want to give access to QBO to the owner or a manager who doesn't actually interact with QBO.
- **Time tracking only** is for employees or subcontractors to add their time. This is an advanced topic and beyond the scope of this book.

We're going to select **Standard User** and then click **<Next>**.

⚙️ **Gear icon** menu → **YOUR COMPANY: Manage users**

Add a new user   ✕

Select access rights

How much access do you want this user to have?   All access

- ◉ All   This user can see and do everything with:
- ○ None
- ○ Limited   ✔ Customers and Sales
    - ☐ Customers   ✔ Suppliers and Purchases
    - ☐ Suppliers

                                                     They can also:

                                                     ✔ Add, edit, and delete employees
                                                     ✔ Change preferences
                                                     ✔ View activity log
                                                     ✔ Create, edit, and delete budgets
                                                     ✔ Add, edit, and delete accounts
                                                     ✔ Make deposits and transfer funds
                                                     ✔ Reconcile accounts and make journal entries
                                                     ✔ View all reports
                                                     ✔ Turn on sales tax (GST/HST, PST, and QST) for the company
                                                     ✔ Change the setup for existing sales tax information
                                                     ✔ Make sales tax adjustments and file sales tax returns
                                                     ✔ Set up multicurrency
                                                     ✔ Perform home currency adjustments
                                                     ✔ Forward receipts and bills from email

(Previous)   (Next)

There are three levels of access rights that you can select:

- ◉ **All** gives access to all functions in QBO.
- ◉ **None** will only give your user access to a very limited range of functions, such as adding their own time sheets.
- ◉ **Limited** gives access to either Customers, Suppliers, or both:

Add a new user   ✕

Select access rights

How much access do you want this user to have?   Customers and suppliers

○ All
○ None   This user can:
● Limited
  ☑ Customers   ✓ Enter estimates, invoices, sales receipts, credit memos, refunds, charges, and credits
  ☑ Suppliers   ✓ Create and delete statements
                                     ✓ Receive payments from customers
                                       ✓ Fill out time sheets for anyone
                                       ✓ Add, edit, and delete customers, suppliers, products, and services
                                       ✓ View customer registers
                                         ✓ View customer and A/R reports
                                         ✓ View supplier and A/P reports
                                         ✓ Enter bills from suppliers
                                         ✓ Pay bills, write and print checks, and view check reports
                                         ✓ Make bills and purchases billable to customers
                                         ✓ Enter cash and credit card purchases

They can't:

✗ Add, edit, and delete accounts and quantity on hand
✗ View bank registers
✗ See total income and expense amounts on Home, Supplier, and Customer pages

[Previous]   [Next]

● **Limited** access is useful for employees or administrators to whom you want give access to select functions but don't want to allow them to see banking information, the ability to edit or delete accounts in the Chart of Accounts, or see reports, including income and Expenses.

Once you have selected either ● **All** or ● **Limited** and checked the functions the user will have access to, click on **<Next>**.

⚙ **Gear icon** menu → **YOUR COMPANY: Manage users**

The next screen shows you some additional permissions with respect to users, company info, and managing subscriptions, that apply to both **All** and **Limited**.

Add a new user   ✕

Select user settings

Do you want this user to add, edit, and remove users?
- ◉ Yes
- ◯ No
- ◯ View only

Do you want this user to edit company info?
- ◉ Yes
- ◯ No

Do you want this user to manage subscriptions?
- ◉ Yes
- ◯ No
- ◯ View only

(Previous)   (Next)

The functionality you provide to your users will depend on their role in the company. You might want an administrator to be able to manage users but not make any changes to the company info or subscriptions to ensure no inadvertent or deliberate manipulation of information. Once you have finished, click **<Next>**.

You would then add your user's contact info.

Add a new user   ✕

What's their contact info?

We'll invite them to create a QuickBooks account and password for access to your company. This invite expires after 30 days.

First name

John

Last name

Watson

Email

watson@shda.com

This will be their user id.

(Previous)   (Save)

Click on **<Save>**, which will send an invitation to the new user. The user would then create their own QBO account and be able to access the aspects of the company file based on the permissions you have granted.

⚙ **Gear icon** menu → **YOUR COMPANY: Manage users**

Accounting firms Tab

To add a new accounting firm, click **[Accounting firms]** and then simply click on
<Invite> and add the information for the accountant. You can add up to two
accountants.

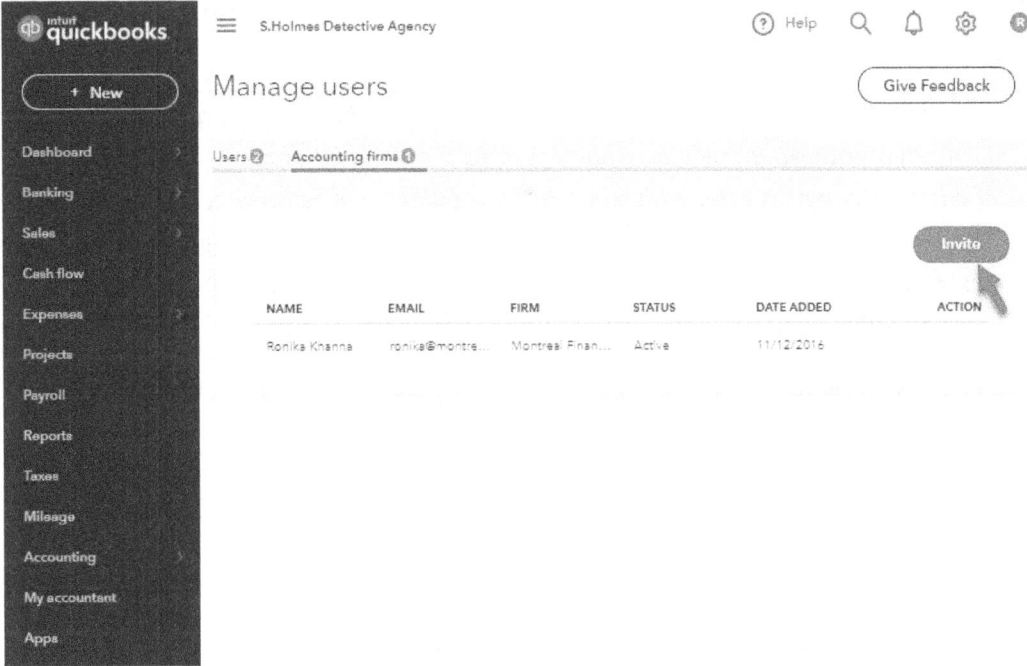

Custom form styles

One of the most used and useful functions of QBO is the ability to send out Invoices to your Customers and clients. See also the section on Customize look and feel.

Before sending out your first invoice, you need to customize the way your invoice is going to look. You can also customize Estimates and Sales Receipts, if applicable.

> ➢ An invoice is effectively a <u>request</u> for payment, while a sales receipt is a <u>proof</u> of payment. An invoice is usually sent to a customer or client indicating when payment is due, which can be immediately (due on receipt) or within a certain number of days such as 30 (Net 30) or 60 (Net 60) days. A sales receipt, conversely, is usually handed over at the time of sale, such as at a retail store or to a handyperson upon completion of work.

If you already have an Invoice format that you like and have used in the past, you can import this into QBO using **Import style**, discussed below. QBO has a detailed list of instructions for importing an existing format that requires that you designate each field on the Invoice to map to the corresponding field in QBO.

Otherwise, you can create a new style within QBO.

> ➢ QBO customization for Invoices is somewhat limited.

To create a new invoice/estimate or sales receipt template, click on the ⚙️**Gear icon** and then **Custom form styles** under **YOUR COMPANY**.

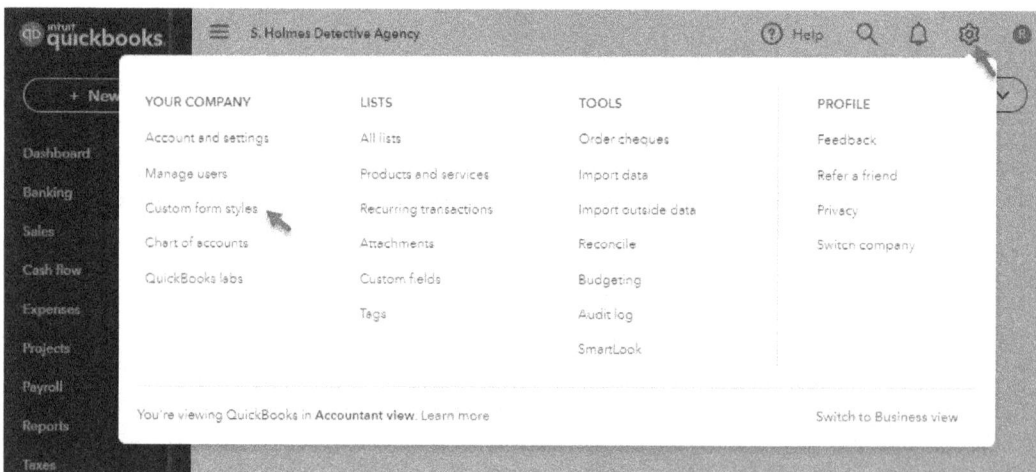

⚙ **Gear icon** menu → **YOUR COMPANY: Custom form styles**

There will likely already be a default style that is auto generated by QBO. If invoice formats aren't important and are simply a means to an end, then you can simply use this as your invoice format.

However, if you would like to give your Invoices some aesthetic appeal and make them your own by adding a logo, fonts, and colours, then you would click on **<New style ▼ >**.

The dropdown menu presents these options:

- Import style is an advanced process and beyond the scope of this book. However, QBO gives you detailed instructions on how to do this.
- Invoice
- Estimate
- Sales receipt

Since the process is the same for all three, we will review how to customize your invoice form.

Clicking on **<New style ▼ >** and selecting Invoice will bring up the following:

You have three tabs here: **[Design]**, **[Content]**, and **[Emails]**.

⚙ **Gear icon** menu → **YOUR COMPANY: Custom form styles**

Design Tab

Create invoices that turn heads and open wallets

| Design | Content | Emails |

My INVOICE Template - 8-9 (77372)

Change up the template

Make logo edits

Splash on some colour

Ff Get choosy with your font

When in doubt, print it out

- **Change up the template** will let you name the template, so that you easily recognize it. This is particularly important when you have more than one template. Since SHDA will use this template to invoice their consulting clients they have named it "SHDA Consultation Invoice". Then select one of the six templates, which can be further customized.

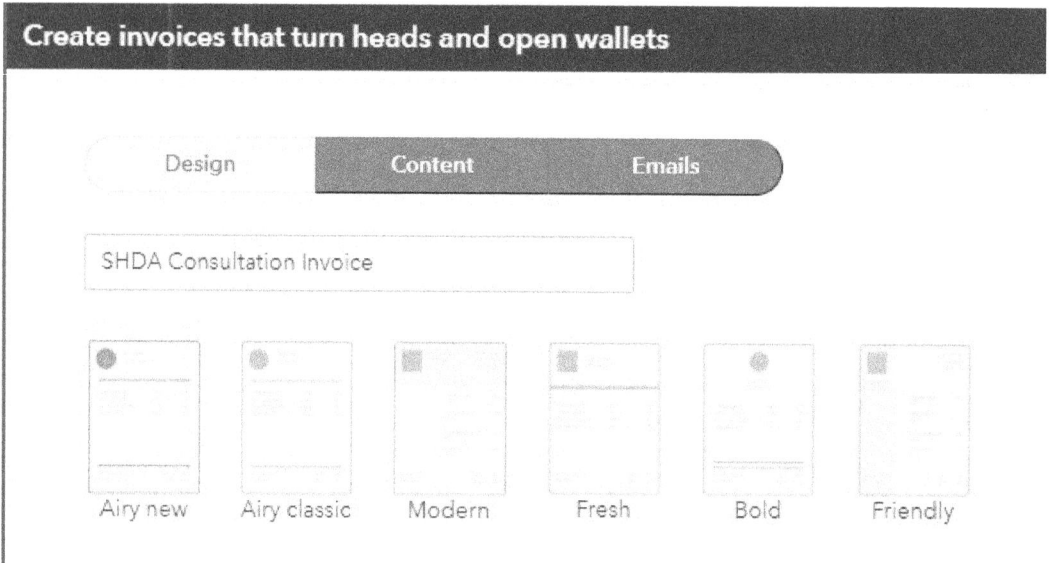

- **Make logo edits** will allow you to add the logo that you might have uploaded when customizing your company settings, or you can add a completely different logo. You can also make the logo **(S)**mall, **(M)**edium, or **(L)**arge (SHDA likes it large), and you can place it where you would like to appear on the Invoice (≡) Left, (≡) Centre, or (≡) Right.

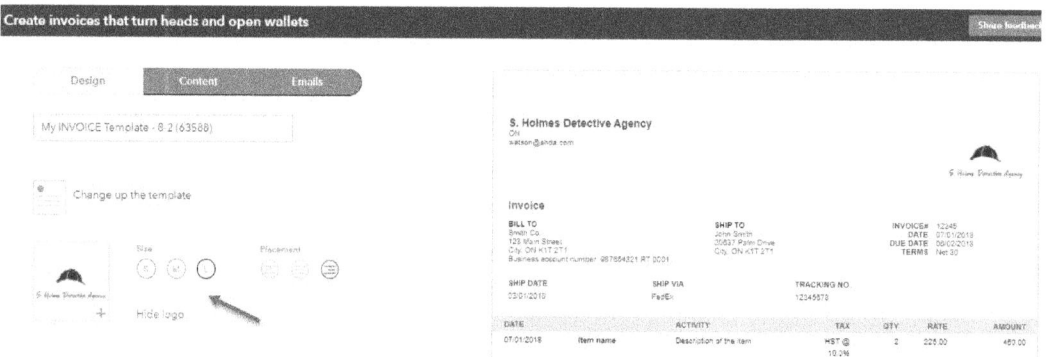

⚙ Gear icon menu → **YOUR COMPANY: Custom form styles**

- **Splash on some colour** will let you choose a colour scheme, which can be one of the pre-selected schemes, or you can add a HTML colour code if you prefer something different or that matches with your business colour scheme.

- **Get choosy with your font** to change the appearance ot the text. QBO only gives you 4 choices at this time:

- **When in doubt, print it to out** to select your print options, which include page margins and the option to use letterhead paper, which will remove your logo.

Content Tab

[Content] is where you can adjust which fields appear on the Invoice by clicking on the ✏ **Pencil icon** that appears in the top right of each of the three sections:

Header

The first section of the Invoice is referred to as the header. Here you can choose which fields appear on your invoice and change the values. For example, if you want to refer to use a different **Business name** than your main one (such as a separate division), you can change it here. Alternatively, you can set up a different **Email**, **Phone** number, **Street address**, etc.

You can also change the form names. For example, QBO does not technically have sales orders. It does however have Estimates, and you can change the name on the sales form from estimate to sales order if this is how you would like it to appear to Customers.

You can choose to display **Shipping**, **Terms**, **Payment method**, etc. If you have set up custom fields, you can also choose where these appear on the form.

Table

This is the body of the Invoice where, similar to above, you can choose to hide or display certain fields such as **Date**, **Product/Service** and related details, **Description**, **Tax**, **Quantity**, etc.

There is also a section that allows you to **Group activity by ▼** , **Show markup on billable expenses**, and **Show billable time**. For example, if you charge a customer for materials, you might show the actual cost plus a specific markup.

Footer

The Footer is the bottom third of the Invoice and can be customized to display certain fields such as **Discount, Deposit, Tax summary**, and **Estimate summary**. The **Tax summary** is useful to show when you charge more than one tax (such as GST and PST).

Message to customer on ▼ allows you to customize a message that will show up on all invoices. QBO gives you some sample text that you can use, or you can create your own.

You can select the font of the messages that will be used from the dropdown.

Finally **Add payment details and footer** lets you enter details relating to payment or anything else you want to include on the footer of your invoice, such as an address or contact detail. You can choose a font and alignment of the message from the dropdown.

Emails Tab

Finally, you can format the **[Emails]** which you send along with your invoice. You can choose to show **Full details** or simply **Summarized details**. **Use greeting** allows you to customize the salutation, while **Message to customer** customizes the text of the email itself. There is also another section where you can customize the message on the **Reminder email** for delinquent Customers. QBO already prepopulates this with a standard message that you can keep or adjust as necessary.

Once you have customized your invoice, don't forget to click on **<Done>**; otherwise, your changes won't be saved!

Chart of accounts

What is a Chart of Accounts?

The Chart of Accounts (COA) is one of the most important aspects of setting up your QBO file. A Chart of Accounts is the structural framework for any business accounting system. It is analogous to a filing system. If you wanted to, you could dump all your documents into one giant file in your filing cabinet (or a file folder on your computer). Of course, if you did do it this way, you would likely have a hard time locating your documents. Alternatively, you could create a series of folders, based on an organizational system that makes sense for you and your business. This type of structure would make it much easier and (as long as you remember your system) much more efficient to find what you are looking for. The more precise your system, the more time you save and the easier your documents become to access. Similarly, a Chart of Accounts is a type of categorization arrangement for your financial data. You slot everything into a category with the ultimate goal of getting financial reports that provides valuable info to the business owner as well as the other stakeholders of the business. It should be noted that while each Chart of Accounts has commonalities and some specific conventions that should be followed, there is no one size fits all. Consequently, it is important to spend some time thinking about a Chart of Accounts that fits the profile of your business.

Components of a Chart of Accounts

Every accounting system uses the same structure:

Balance Sheet

- Assets
- Current assets such as your bank accounts, Accounts Receivable, Inventory, and short-term deposits and investments that will be utilized in the short term.
- Long term assets are generally investments that are held for the long term.
- Capital assets are property and intangibles that have a useful life beyond one year, such as computers, furniture, trademarks, and patents.
- Liabilities

- Current liabilities include Accounts Payable owing to Suppliers, taxes payable, credit card balances, and anything that is owing within a year.
- Long term liabilities refers to debt and amounts owing that are due after a period exceeding one year.
- Equity
- Shareholder or owner contributions to company for which they received shares of the business.
- Retained earnings, which are the accumulated profits/losses of the company since its inception.

Profit and Loss Statement

- Sales, which include products and service revenues.
- Cost of Goods Sold.
- Direct costs of manufacturing products or incurred for services such as materials, shipping, customs duties, packaging, and direct labour.
- Expenses, which include indirect costs such as salaries, rent, marketing, office expenses, travel, etc. that are part of business activities.
- Other Income and Expenses.
- Other revenues such investment income or expenses that do not relate directly to the primary business operations.

Questions to Ask before Setting Up Your Chart of Accounts

Before setting up your Chart of Accounts, ideally you should go through an interview process for your business to determine the best structure. Some examples of questions include:

- Do you sell products? Services? Both?
- Do you have distinct Customers in different Locations?
- Do you have different divisions?
- Are your services or products sold on a recurring basis, or are they a one-time purchase?
- Do you have different types of product or service lines?
- Do you spend a lot on marketing, or research and development, or another expense where you want to see a more detailed breakdown?
- Do you have different types of debt and/or investments?

⚙ **Gear icon** menu → **YOUR COMPANY: Chart of accounts**

By analyzing your business and the type of data analysis that will help you with your business decision making, you can determine how you want to organize your data. For example, if you have a product-based business, you could set up sales with the product lines as sub-categories. You would also want to reflect your Cost of Goods Sold which includes purchases of materials, shipping, packaging, and other direct costs relating to your business.

If your products or services are better distinguished by location or division, it might make sense to use one of these categories to track them.

If you sell recurring items as well as one-off services, you might organize your sales into these two categories, or you might choose to have one line each for products vs services.

Significant expenses relating to advertising, or research and development, might warrant a detailed set of sub-accounts.

Limitations and Size of the Chart of Accounts

Similar to a filing system, there are limitations in how you structure a Chart of Accounts. You can and should have both accounts and sub-accounts; however, too many accounts can be counter productive. It is important to have a clear idea of the distinction between accounts, as there are numerous transactions that could belong to more than one account. If you have sales by customer but also product line, you will have difficulty determining which account it should be allocated to, and your Chart of Accounts will not be very useful. This is one of the more difficult aspects when setting up a Chart of Accounts—ultimately you have to identify what type of structure gives you the most meaningful view of your data. The good news is that you don't have to give up reporting functionality; QBO has many different ways of querying your data. For example, you can create reports by customer, or products, or vendors. Additionally, you can track different Locations or product lines using a tagging system.

Chart of Accounts vs Other Types of Tagging

Every time you create a transaction in QBO, there are multiple fields in which you can enter data. A typical sales transaction will have the customer, date of transaction, invoice number, item, amount, and sales tax code. There are also custom fields that can be created for elements such as sales reps, special discounts codes, etc. Reports can then be generated for any data entered into a field. For example, you can create reports that show you all your sales by customer or date or within a certain location (or a combination of some or all of these). As such, thought has to be given as to whether certain categories belong more appropriately on the Chart of Accounts—or is being able to create a report for these queries sufficient? For example, since you can see your products sales by using a separate report, you don't necessarily need each product on the Chart of Accounts. Rather you could have a more general product or service line that combines several products and/or services as explained in the product and services section.

Should You Use Account Numbers?

QBO allows you to assign numbers to each account as explained here. The advantage of this is that it allows for additional sorting and a better understanding of your accounts at a glance. A typical accounting system uses the following numbers:

- Assets start at 1000(0)
- Liabilities start at 2000(0)
- Equity starts at 3000(0)
- Sales start at 4000(0)
- Cost of Goods Sold starts at 5000(0)
- Expenses start at 6000(0)
- Other Income and Expenses can be 7000(0) and 8000(0) respectively

If you are a small business and expect to remain so for the foreseeable future, it might make sense to start with 4 digits. However, if you expect to scale quickly, you would want to start out with 5 digits right away as this gives you more flexibility.

For example, you could use 4000 to denote all your sales. However, you would want to have sub-categories (discussed below) you could use 4100 for services and 4200 for products. If you have 3 types of services and 3 types of products you could use 4110, 4120, and 4130, and 4210, 4220, and 4230. This allows the reader of the Financial Statements to instantly know that 4230 is a subcategory of 4200 which is a subcategory of 4000.

When using numbers, it is good practice to anticipate future accounts; leaving room between numbers allows for more flexibility in the future as your business changes and grows.

⚙ **Gear icon** menu → **YOUR COMPANY: Chart of accounts**

Should You Use Sub-Accounts?

Unless you have a very simple business with one service and a handful of expenses, it is a good idea to structure your COA with master and sub-accounts. The benefit of this is that it allows you to see a main account broken down into its various sub-components, therefore allowing for better visibility of data. By creating sub-accounts of one category, you can see both the total by the category and the total by each account. Sub-accounts should be used when there are enough transactions to warrant a separate account. For example, you could use sub-accounts for sales if you want to see total sales by a specific product line. You might decide that you want to track marketing expenses by its components such as advertising, costs of attending shows, costs of printing marketing materials, etc. Conversely, if you have an Expense category for rent that you pay monthly for your premises and another Expense that you pay once a year for a storage facility, it might not make sense to have a sub-account for the storage facility since this does not provide much in the way of useful information.

Update Your Accounts as Your Business Evolves

Every business evolves over time, and it is rare for a growing business to get their Chart of Accounts right the first time. You can add accounts, move transactions, create sub-accounts, and delete accounts. You can also merge accounts in some situations. QBO allows you to remove accounts that are no longer in use; however, it should be noted that an account in QBO is never actually deleted. Instead, it is made "inactive". The upside is that you can always reactivate the account. The downside is that if you view your Chart of Accounts, including all inactive accounts, it can get a bit cluttered. If an account has a balance, then it will still show up on your Financial Statements, usually with a "deleted" description next to it. It is good practice to have a process for how Charts of Accounts are set up and by whom, and that they follow a logical framework to avoid inconsistencies.

Set Up Your Chart of Accounts for Your Business Rather than Your Accountant

Many businesses will ask their accountants to help set up their Chart of Accounts. While accountants are the best people to ask about the set up, it is important to note that accountants might focus on setting it up to optimize their own tax or Financial Statements reporting rather than addressing the needs of the business. As such, if you are using an accountant, it is important to contemplate what type of reporting is important to you as the business owner and to communicate your needs clearly—and firmly—to your accountant.

Understanding the Chart of Accounts in QBO

Note that QBO also refers to accounts as "categories" when entering transactions. As such account and category are often (but not always) interchangeable.

Go the ⚙ **Gear icon** and select **Chart of accounts**, under **YOUR COMPANY**.

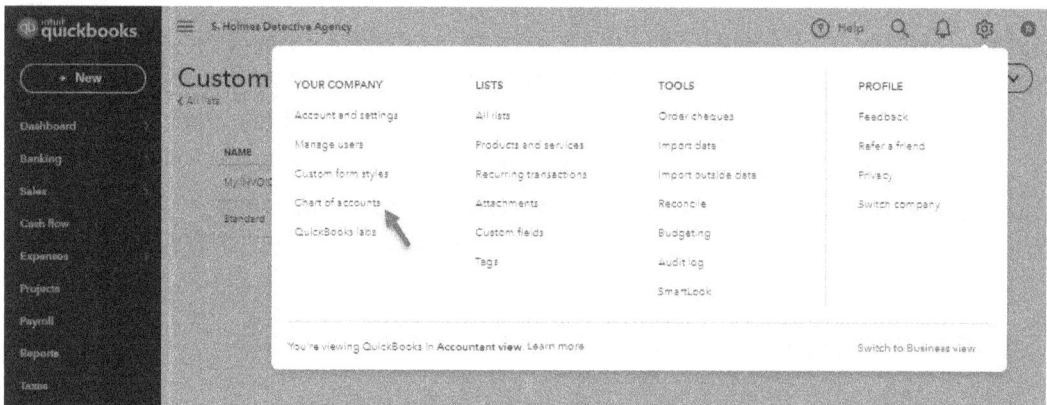

> ⇅ *You can also access the COA by going to **Accounting >** on the **Left-hand Navigation Bar** and selecting **Chart of Accounts**.*

You will be taken to the following screen which shows you all the accounts that have been set up.

⚙ **Gear icon** menu → **YOUR COMPANY: Chart of accounts**

Let's look at the headers:

NAME	TYPE ▲	DETAIL TYPE	TAX RATE	QUICKBOOKS BALANCE	BANK BALANCE	ACTION
Checking (6482)	Bank	Chequing		60,801.73	6,267.40	Account history ▼
Accounts Receivable (	Accounts receivab...	Accounts Receiva...		10,203.62		Account history ▼
Inventory Asset	Current assets	Inventory	Exempt	17,000.00		Account history ▼
Uncategorized Asset	Current assets	Other current assets		0.00		Account history ▼
Undeposited Funds	Current assets	Undeposited Funds		0.00		Account history ▼
Investments	Long-term Assets	Investments	Out of Scope	20,000.00		Account history ▼
Accounts Payable (A/P	Accounts payable...	Accounts Payable...		5,763.00		Account history ▼
Amex Gold	Credit Card	Credit Card		6,742.67	-1,576.68	Account history ▼

- **NAME** is the name that you have given to the account. This should be descriptive so that it is easy to locate.
- **TYPE** represents which broad category the account falls into. The different types of accounts available in QBO are as follows:
- **Bank** accounts or cash on hand.
- **Accounts receivable** (AR) specifically pertains to amounts owing from Customers. There is usually only one AR account for each currency. To see all amounts owing by Customers you would go to a separate report, called the A/R Aging Summary.
- **Current assets** are any type of assets that are not specifically bank or accounts receivable, such as Inventory, short term deposits, or Expenses that have been prepaid.
- **Property, plant and equipment** generally refers to depreciable assets such as furniture, equipment, machinery, and computers.
- **Long-term Assets** are usually held on to for longer than one year, such as investments, long term rental deposits, investments in real estate, amounts paid for trademarks or patents, etc.

- **Accounts payable** (AP) specifically pertains to amounts owing from Suppliers. Similar to AR, there is usually only one AP account for each currency. To see all amounts owing to Suppliers you would access the AP Aging Summary.
- Credit Card
- **Other Current Liabilities** includes accounts that are not Accounts Payable nor credit cards, such as taxes payable, accrued liabilities (liabilities that you know that you will have in the future but have not yet received a Bill), and short-term loans. Shareholder loans also often fall into this category.
- **Long-term Liabilities** are those that are only payable after one year, such as bank loans.
- **Equity** refers to amounts that are contributed by the owner for a sole proprietorship or shareholders in a corporation, also referred to as share capital. This section also includes dividends paid to shareholders and retained earnings.
- **Income** includes your sales and revenue accounts that directly relate to your business.
- **Other income** are tangential sources of income such as interest on investments.
- Cost of Goods Sold
- Expenses
- **Other expenses** include Expenses that are unusual or tangential to your business.
- **DETAIL TYPE** provides a list of different types of account available for each broad category described above. You would simply select the detail type that most closely resembles the account that you are adding. The detail is not really important (I have yet to use it for any purpose), as long as you select something that seems appropriate, you should be fine.
- **TAX RATE** refers to the sales tax code that applies to the particular account. This is simply a default selection that can be changed for each transaction. Some accounts will have tax codes that apply in most cases, such as bank charges that is an Expense that will almost always be tax exempt. Other tax codes will depend on the nature of the transactions, e.g., some travel will be exempt while others will have HST or GST. If the tax code is subject to change, you can leave this blank.

- **QUICKBOOKS BALANCE** is the balance in the account per QBO.
- **BANK BALANCE** refers to accounts that are linked to the bank account and regularly downloading transactions and represent the balance per the bank itself. If this is different from QBO, then the accounts should be reviewed and reconciled.
- **ACTION** provides you with four options that you can perform for each account:

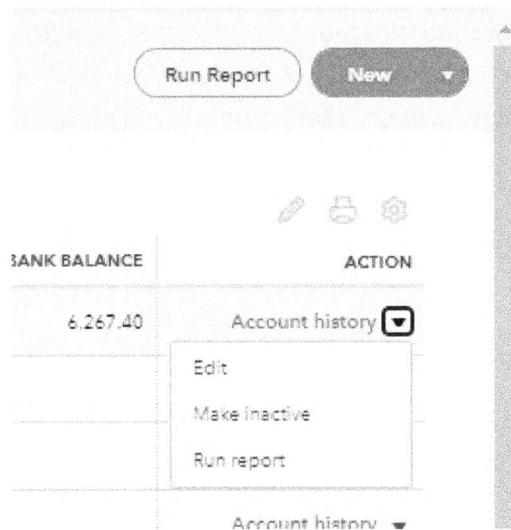

- Account history takes you to a different view of the chart of accounts called the account register. This is a feature that is available in QBDT but is rarely used in QBO.
- Edit allows you to change the details of the account such as the **Name**, **Type**, **Tax code**, etc.
- Make inactive lets you "delete" or make an account that you no longer use inactive. Note that QBO never actually deletes accounts. It simply removes them from view.
- Run report allows you to generate a report for the specific account. This will give you a report view for the transactions in the account based on the date range on the top of the report, which can then be changed. This report can also be found in the reports section and referred to as the transactions by account.

Creating a Chart of Accounts in QBO for the First Time

When creating a Chart of Accounts for the first time, you have several options:

1. You can create an account manually from the **Chart of Accounts** interface (discussed below).
2. If you already have a Chart of Accounts outside of QBO, you can import it by clicking on the ⚙ **Gear icon** and selecting **Import data** under **TOOLS**. This is an advanced topic and beyond the scope of this book.
3. You can create accounts as and when needed, directly when you are entering transactions. Whenever QBO asks for a category, it allows you to select from a dropdown or create a new account directly.

Create a New Account

To create a new account, click on **<New ▾ >** on the top right-hand side of the Chart of Accounts screen:

⚙ **Gear icon** menu → **YOUR COMPANY: Chart of accounts**

This will bring up the following **Account** screen:

- **Account Type▼**, **Detail Type▼**, and **Name** are discussed above and are required fields.
- **Description** is optional and is only necessary if you want to see internal notes describing the nature of the account.
- **Is sub-account** allows you to make an account a sub-account. To create a sub-account, that then forms part of a parent account, you would select the parent account from the **Enter parent account▼** dropdown.

❖ *For example, if your business pays rent at more than one location, you might want different accounts for each location, but that can also all be seen as part of rent expense. In this case you would choose the rent account as the master account and each location as a sub-account.*

- **Default tax code▾** is discussed above.
- **Balance** should only be entered if there is a balance in the account due to a transfer from another accounting system. Even then, it is often better to enter opening balances as a Journal Entry rather than entering them in this section.

Import a Chart of Accounts

This is an advanced topic and beyond the scope of this book.

Enter an Account Directly from the Transaction Window

Accounts in QBO can be entered directly in almost any transaction window, including invoices, bills, expenses and journal entries. For details on how to do this please refer to the adding an expense section.

QuickBooks labs

This is an area where QBO posts experimental features that you can test and play around with. They regularly update and change the features here, some of which become available in the regular version of QBO while others, that don't work well, are retired.

LISTS

Lists are the foundation upon which your accounting file is built in QBO and is part of customizing your setup. The information provided in each list is what QBO uses to provide structure to your day-to day-transactions. When a list is properly customized, transactions can be entered and analyzed in a meaningful way.

Lists are usually accessed by going to the ⚙️**Gear icon**. There is however some duplication of menus, so you will frequently see the same list in several different areas. I will be reviewing each list in the order in which it is presented in the ⚙️**Gear icon** menu. Where there is duplication, I will be referencing the chapter where the details about the specific list are presented.

All lists

To access the master list of lists, go to the ⚙️**Gear icon** and click on **All lists** under **LISTS**.

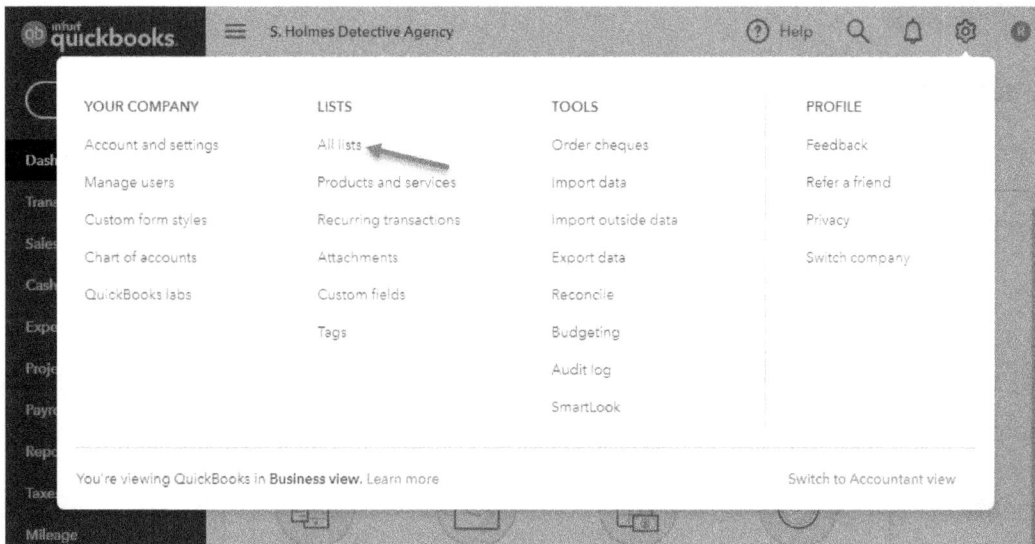

This will take you to the following screen which shows you all the lists available for customization in QBO:

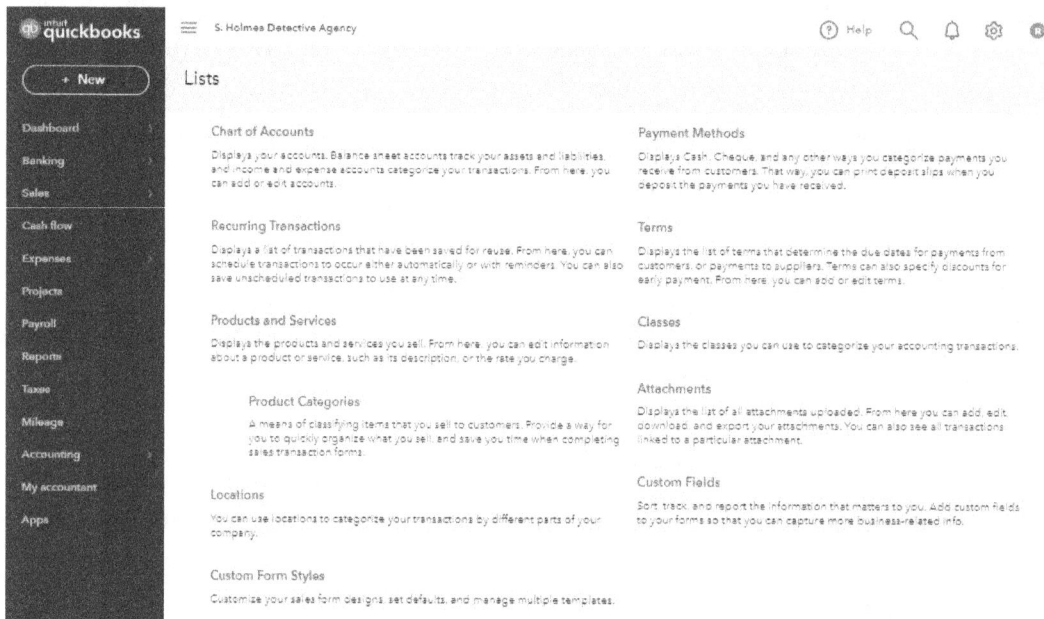

Chart of Accounts

Please see section on Chart of Accounts.

Recurring Transactions

Please see section on Recurring Transactions.

Products and Services

Please see section on Products and Services.

Locations (Plus)

Businesses that sell their products or services might want to track Locations. There are many ways this type of tracking can be used. This is an advanced topic and beyond the scope of this book.

Check out our article for more information on Locations and Classes.

Custom Form Styles

Please see section on Custom Form Styles.

Payment Methods

Most businesses allow for more than one payment method. This can be tracked here and is used mainly for reporting purposes to see how your Customers have paid you. To access Payment Methods, click on the ⚙ **Gear icon** and then **All lists** under **LISTS**, and then **Payment Methods.** QBO usually prepopulates this with the following:

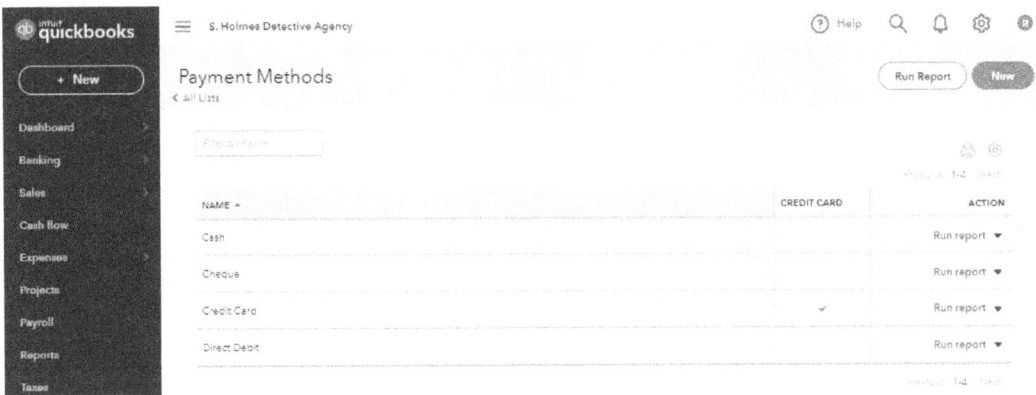

- **NAME**
  - **Cash**
  - **Cheque**
  - **Credit Card**
  - **Direct Debit**

Other payment methods that can be added include:

  - **Paypal**
  - **Stripe**
  - **Wire transfer**
  - **Pre-authorized debit**

To add a new payment method, click on **<New>**. The following window will open.

- Add the name of the payment method. Check the box ☑**This is a credit card** if appropriate. Once you have added the name of the payment method, click on **<Save>**.

New Payment Method ✕

* Name

☐ This is a credit card

Cancel   Save

- The payment method can now be added to various forms and will be available as a dropdown on Invoices. You can then create reports to see a summary and details of how Customers have paid you.

Classes (Plus)

The next option in **All lists** is **Classes**. This is similar to Locations, except that reporting for Classes is limited to the Profit and Loss statement. Businesses that sell their products or services might want to track Classes or Locations or both. This is another powerful reporting feature and are many different ways this type of tracking can be used. This is an advanced topic and beyond the scope of this book.

Check out our article for more information on Locations and Classes.

Terms

The next option in **All lists** is **Terms**. Further to our discussion about **Terms** in the set up of sales form content section, businesses that invoice their clients typically allow them a certain amount of time to pay. This is usually reflected on the Invoice itself along with a due date. There is an accounting convention for terms, examples of which are:

⚙ **Gear icon** menu → **LISTS: All lists**

- Upon Receipt: Payment is due on the day that you send out the Invoice
- **Net 7**, **Net 21**, **Net 30**, **60**, or **90:** Payment is due within the number of days indicated after "Net". Net 7 is one week, Net 21 three weeks, while Net 30 is one month etc.
- **2/10 Net 30:** A variation of an Invoice that is due within 30 days that offers a discount for early payment of 2% if paid within 10 days.

> ➤ *Terms can be anything that you want them to be and are often decided based on your own cash flow needs and the amount of time that you think is reasonable for your Customers. Each customer can have their own payment terms.*

How to Set Up Terms

Select terms by clicking the ⚙ **Gear icon** and then **LISTS: All Lists** → **Terms**. You will be taken to the screen below:

You will see the terms that are already set up. Click **<New>** to open the **New Term** window.

We will set up a term with the **Name** "15 MFI" indicating that an Invoice is ⦿**Due by certain day of the month**, specifically the 15th **day of the month** following the invoice date. For example, if the Invoice is sent April 20, the payment is due May 15. However, if the Invoice is sent on May 1, it will be due on June 15, which is the month following the date of the Invoice. "15 MFI" is the conventional accounting jargon for this type of payment term.

Simply click on **<Save>** and this term will become available as an option, which you can then enter on your Invoices or Bills.

Attachments

Please see section on Attachments.

Custom Fields

Please see section on Custom Fields.

Products and services

Further to the introduction about Products and Services, every business sells at least one product or service, and many businesses have multiple.

Setting up a product or services requires you to think about:

- What types of products or services you will be selling to Customers.
- How you want the name of the product/service to show up on the Invoices you send to Customers.
- What type of reporting you would like for the product/service.
- Whether you have Inventory, and if so whether you want to track it separately.
- Whether you would like to set up separate products/services for similar types, or will a customized description be sufficient.

> ❖ *In our case study, SHDA sells consulting services and magnifying glasses. Which means they have at least one service and one product.*
>
> ◆ *They also plan to have an Inventory of completed magnifying glasses that includes their most popular sizes and lens options.*
>
> ◆ *Additionally, they have an Inventory of parts that go into making the magnifying glasses.*
>
> ◆ *The consulting services are offered primarily to government agencies, including the police, but also some private clients.*
>
> ◆ *Watson and Holmes have decided to set up products for their most popular magnifying glasses for now. As demand grows, and they are able to identify what is popular enough to keep in stock, they will update their product listing.*
>
> ◆ *For their services, they believe that having two types of service, one for all government agencies and another for all private clients, is sufficient for tracking and reporting purposes at this juncture. As the business grows, they will revisit this.*
>
> ◆ *Product categories allow for additional grouping of individual Products and Services. This is optional.*

- SHDA will use two product categories for their magnifying glasses, which are hand-held magnifiers and stand magnifiers.

- Currently there is no need for categories for their services.

How to Set Up a Product or Service

> ➤ Note that Inventory tracking and management is only available with the **Plus** version of QBO.

Go to the ⚙️ **Gear icon** and click on **LISTS: Products and services**:

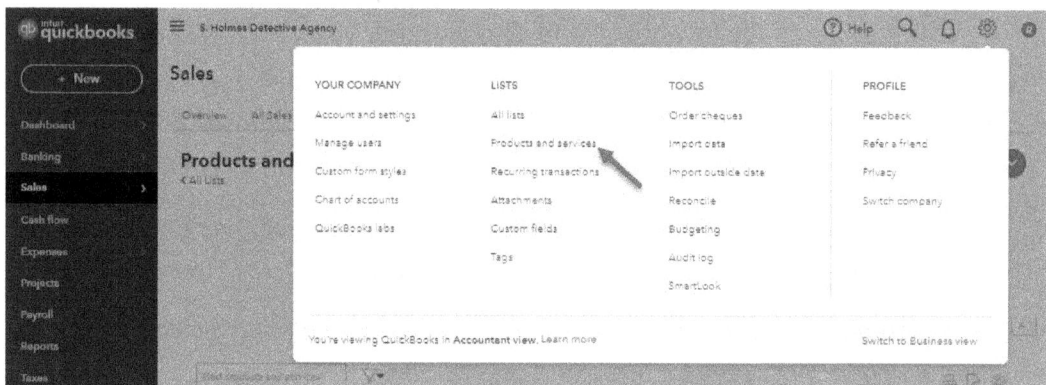

> ↻ You may also access the same screen by clicking **Left-hand Navigation Bar →
> Sales >** (or **Invoicing >**) → **Products and Services**.

You will be taken to the following screen. With the Inventory module (**Plus** version of QBO), you will see an icon with products that have low stock or are out of stock.

⚙️ Gear icon menu → LISTS: Products and services

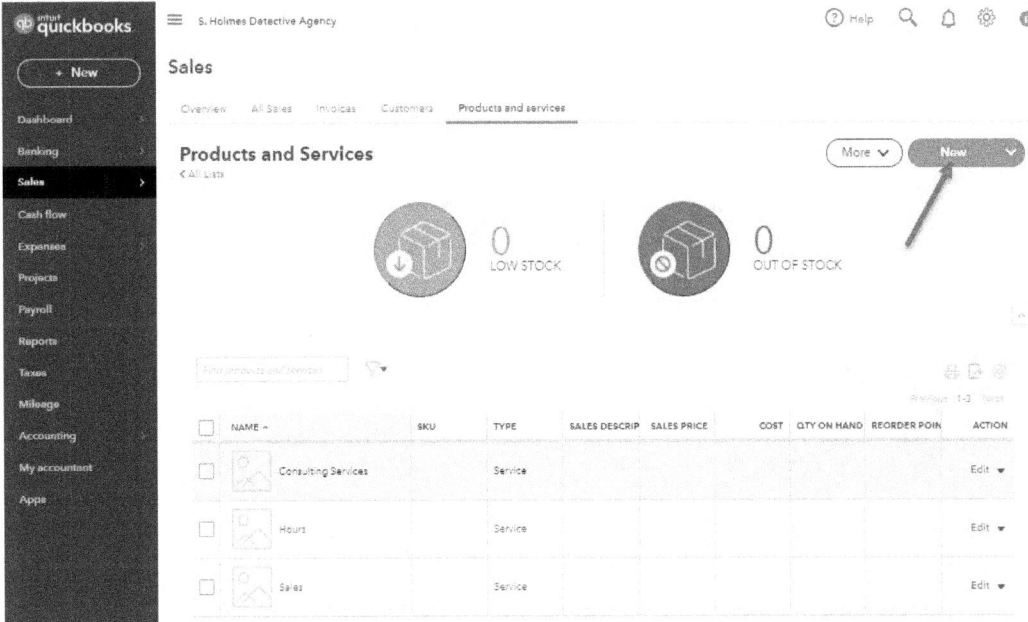

Click on **<New ▼>**. This will open a different menu, depending on your version of QBO.

Product/Service information options if you are using EasyStart or Essentials:

Product/Service information   ✕

Non-inventory
Products you buy and/or sell but don't need to (or can't) track quantities of, for example, nuts and bolts used in an installation.

Service
Services that you provide to customers, for example, landscaping or tax preparation services.

Bundle
A collection of products and/or services that you sell together, for example, a gift basket of fruit, cheese, and wine.

Product/Service information options if you are using Plus:

Product/Service information ✕

Inventory
Products you buy and/or sell and that you track quantities of.

Non-inventory
Products you buy and/or sell but don't need to (or can't) track quantities of, for example, nuts and bolts used in an installation.

Service
Services that you provide to customers, for example, landscaping or tax preparation services.

Bundle
A collection of products and/or services that you sell together, for example, a gift basket of fruit, cheese, and wine.

We will discuss the features included in EasyStart and Essentials first, and then we'll discuss the additional feature found only in Plus.

Non-inventory

Non-inventory allows you to track quantities of physical goods that you buy or sell, mostly for reporting purposes. Unlike **Inventory, Non-inventory** does not allow you to track the quantity that you currently have in stock. This is particularly relevant for product-based businesses that don't really need to track Inventory or service-based businesses that occasionally sell products.

> ❖ *SHDA occasionally buys audio recording devices (bugs) for use on its jobs. They want to be able to invoice the clients for the bugs, see the quantity purchased, and how many they sell, but don't really need to track the quantity they have in stock.*

Clicking on **Non-inventory** will bring up the following screen:

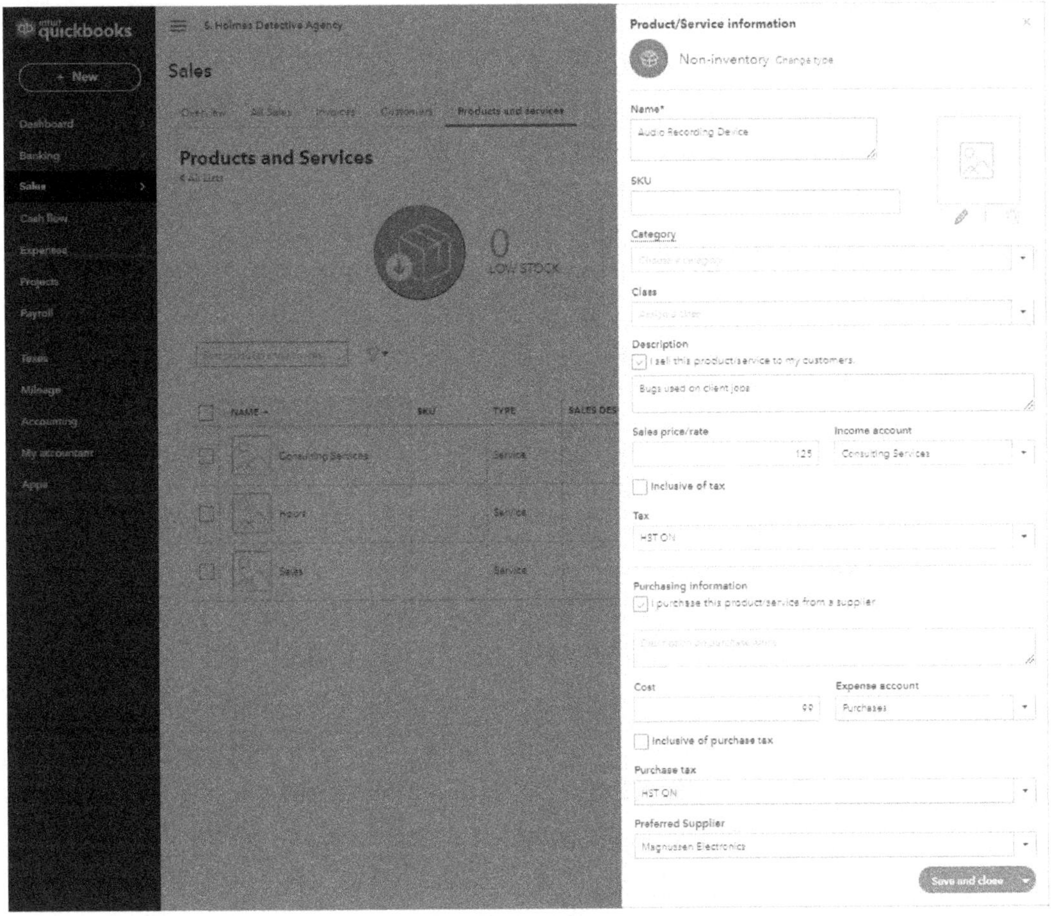

- **Name** of the item should be specific and recognizable.
- **Image** lets you click on the ✏ **Pencil icon** to upload a picture. Click the 🗑 **Trash icon** to delete the picture if you change your mind.
- **SKU** (stock keeping unit) is usually relevant for Inventory items when you have a number of products. Since SHDA only has a couple of these types of products, no SKU is necessary.
- **Category▼** is a way of grouping Non-inventory items that are similar. It isn't necessary to create an additional grouping here since there are only a few Non-inventory items.
- **Class▼** is another grouping mechanism and is the beyond the scope of this book.
- ☑ **I sell this product/service to my customers**, when checked, allows you enter a **Description** of the item that will then automatically appear on sales Invoices and Estimates.
- **Sales price/rate** allows you to pre-set a price or rate for the specific item. This will also pre-populate on sales Invoices and Estimates; however, this can always be changed directly on the Invoice or estimate.
- **Income account▼** refers to the account that the product or service is assigned to. You can create multiple Products and Services that all feed into a small number of accounts on your Chart of Accounts.
- **Tax▼** represents the tax code which is most commonly associated with the sale of this item. In this case, since most of SHDA's clients are in Ontario, they have selected **HST On** as the default tax code.
- **I purchase this product/service from a supplier**, when checked, opens up a field below in which you can enter a description of the product that you purchase. The description will automatically populate on Bills and Expenses when you enter this product.
- **Cost** is how much the product costs from the supplier.
- **Expense account▼** lets you select the account to which this item should be allocated, which will then prepopulate when entering a Bill or Expense.
- **Purchase tax▼** is the tax code of the supplier.
- **Preferred Supplier▼** indicates from whom you mostly purchase the item.

Click **<Save and close▼ >** when you have completed the above.

Service

Service items have the same fields as **Non-inventory** items. The only difference, conceptually, is that **Non-inventory** items usually relate to physical goods, while **Service** items are intangible. An example of a **Service** item can be seen below:

In the service example, SHDA has not set a **Sales price/rate**, since it varies depending on the client. Instead, the price of the service will be set directly on the Invoice. Similarly, the **Description** is usually different for each client, so this field has been left blank and will be entered directly on the Invoice. Finally, services usually don't have **Purchasing information** unless you are directly subcontracting a service, in which case you can complete this information similar to our example for **Non-inventory**.

Bundle

Bundle allows you to group certain Inventory items together that you can then sell as one item.

Product/Service information   ✕

👕 Bundle   Change type

Name*

> Private Consulting Package

SKU

Description

> *Description on sales forms*

Products/services included in the bundle

☑ Display bundle components when printing or sending transactions

PRODUCT/SERVICE	QTY	
Consulting Services	1	🗑
Audio Recording Device Bugs used on client jobs	1	🗑
		🗑

+ Add lines

Save and close ▾

⚙ **Gear icon** menu → **LISTS: Products and services**

In addition to the **Name**, **SKU**, and **Description** fields that are the same as on a **Non-inventory** item, there is an additional field called **PRODUCT/SERVICE**. This field allows you to combine a selection of existing Products and Services to create a new item known as a **Bundle**.

☑ **Display bundle components when printing or sending transactions**, when checked, allows you to show the components of the **Bundle** on the invoice to customers. If not checked, the item will simply be reflected as "Private Consulting Package", which is the **Name** of the **Bundle**.

Inventory (Plus)

The fields available for **Inventory** items are the same as for a **Non-inventory** item, plus some additional fields. Below is an example of a completed **Inventory** item:

- **Image** allows you to include a photo of the item for all **Products and Services**. Here, SHDA has clicked on the ✏ **Pencil icon** to upload a picture of the magnifying glass for this inventory item for their reference.
- **Category ▼** is important for SHDA since they sell several types of products. As such they have created a category which will allow them to group their products by type.

Additional fields include:

- **Initial quantity on hand*** represents the number of this type of product that you already have. This is necessary to properly indicate the reorder point.
- **As of date*** is the date at which you entered the quantity that you have on hand. Going forward, all purchases and sales of this product will be added to or deducted from Inventory.
- **Reorder point** is a powerful Inventory feature that allows you to enter a remaining quantity at which you need to reorder more. QBO will notify you that you are at your reorder point, which prompts you to go ahead and manufacture or order the item.

> ➤ *When you are tracking Inventory, it is essential that you enter the item when making purchases on the Bill and when selling the item on the Invoice. This is necessary to ensure proper tracking of the Inventory.*

- **Inventory asset account ▼** is the account on your Balance Sheet in which movements in Inventory will be reflected. The Balance Sheet always reflects the amount of Inventory on hand, at cost (the amount you paid for it) as of the date on the Balance Sheet. When an item is purchased, it is added to the Inventory account while when an item is sold it is deducted from the Inventory asset account.

All other information is the same as a **Non-inventory** item.

Please refer to chapters on creating Invoices and Bills to see how Products and Services work in conjunction with transactions.

Recurring transactions

A recurring transaction is an automation that is available for transactions that are entered frequently. This applies to Invoices, Bills, Expenses, and journal entries and can help save time and tedious data entry. Once you create a recurring transaction, QBO will automatically enter it on a date specified in the setup. You can also indicate to automatically email an Invoice to a customer.

Since this will make more sense once you have created some transactions, we have discussed it a bit later in the book. Please refer to section below on recurring transactions.

Attachments

The next option in **LISTS** is **Attachments**. QBO allows you to upload source or information files for specific transactions, which we will discuss in Invoices and Bills below. There are a number of files that you can attach to a transaction such as:

- Actual Bills received from Suppliers when entering Bills.
- Purchase orders from Customers for Invoices.
- Time tracking information for an Invoice.
- Credit card receipt for expenses.
- Image of product that might accompany Invoices.
- Photo of item in Inventory.

This section lists all files that have been attached to transactions, specifies the transaction, and allows you to preview or download the attachment.

⚙ **Gear icon** menu → **LISTS: Attachments**

To access the list of attachments, click on the ⚙ **Gear icon**, then **LISTS:
Attachments.** You will see the following screen which shows you all transactions
with attachments:

1.   **Drag/drop files here** into the box, or click 📎 **Attachments icon** to add an
     attachment directly from your computer.

2.   <Batch actions ▼ > allows you to:

     •   Export all or a selection of attachments to a Zip file.
     •   Create invoice from a selected attachment.
     •   Create expense from a selected attachment.

3.   **Download** ▼ a specific attachment. Additionally, by clicking the dropdown
     arrow, you can:

     •   Edit the details of the attachment including the file name and add some
         notes
     •   Delete the attachment
     •   Create invoice from the attachment
     •   Create expense from the attachment

Custom fields (Plus)

We first discussed custom fields in the Customize Your Setup: Sales Tab. In both the Essentials and Plus versions you can add up to 3 custom fields on sales Invoices. However, in Plus, this functionality is expanded so that you can have up to 12 custom fields per form (including Invoices, Estimates, and Purchase Orders). This is one more way of gleaning insights into your business by enhancing your ability to report on custom fields.

To create a custom field, go to the ⚙️ **Gear icon** and click on **LISTS: Custom fields**. Click on **<Add custom field>**. Then, in the pop-up window, enter the name and check the sales forms on which you would like the custom field to appear. Once done click on **<Save>**.

Once you have created a custom field, it will appear in this section and can then be edited. New custom fields can be added when needed.

CUSTOM FIELD NAME	SALES RECEIPT	INVOICE	ESTIMATE	CREDIT MEMO	REFUND RECEIPT	PURCHASE ORDER	ACTIONS
Sales Reps	✓	✓	✓	✓	✓	✓	Edit ⌄

Tags (Essentials and Plus)

Tags are another tracking mechanism available in QBO, which allow you to create reports for transactions that have a specific tag attached to them. The field for tags appears automatically on sales forms (Invoices, Estimates. Etc.). While they do not automatically appear on Bills and Expenses, they can be activated in the section on Bills and Expenses in Accounts and settings , which will create a field where you can enter a tag and create reports.

How to Create a Tag

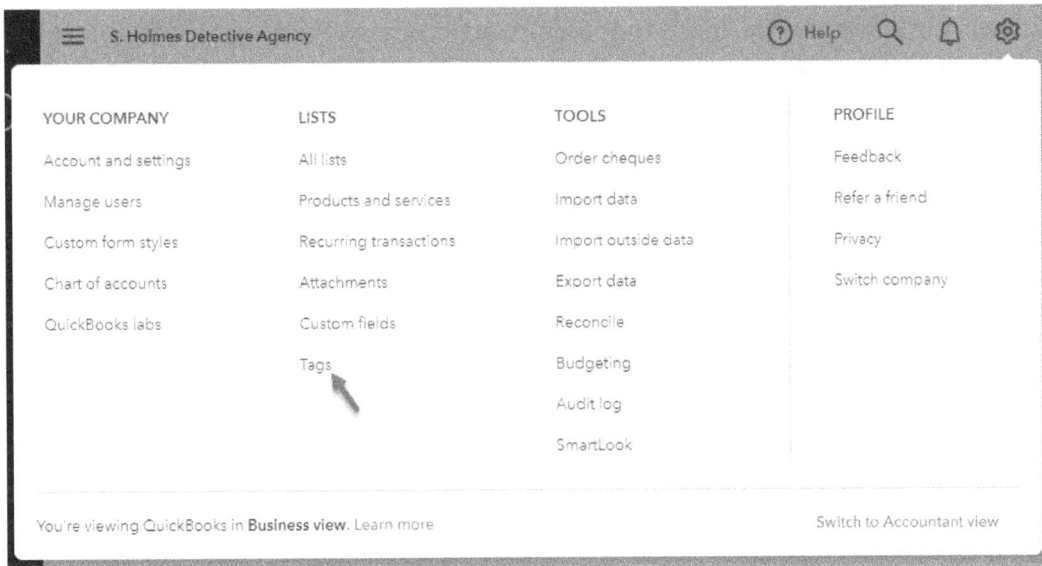

Click on the ⚙ **Gear icon**. Select **LISTS: Tags**. You will be taken to the screen below:

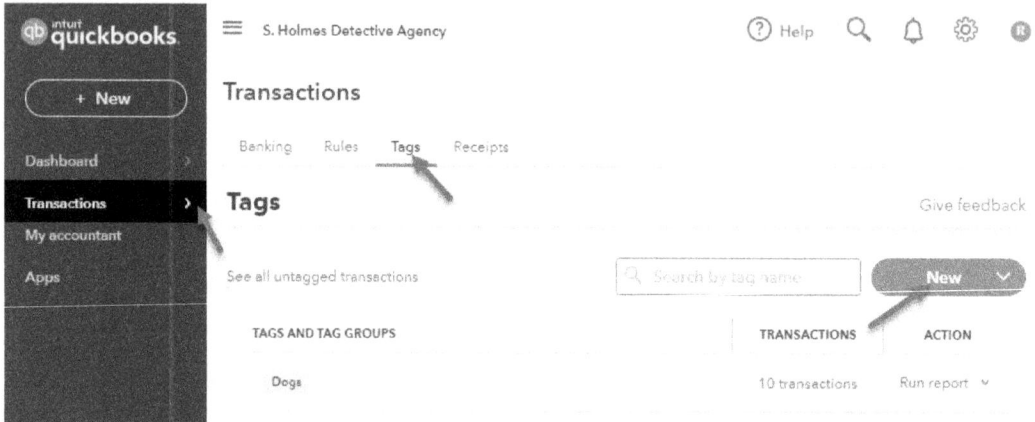

You will note that the link leads to the **Transactions >** (or **Banking >**) section, which is where the **Tags** interface is located. Here you can see a list of all tags that have been created. You can also run a report directly from here of transactions that have been tagged. Additionally, you can run a report for all untagged transactions, which is useful, if you want to identify transactions that should be tagged.

There is a limit of 300 tags. You can also create **Tag Groups** that bundle sub tags under a main tag.

To create a new tag, click on **<New▼>**. This window will open:

You will be prompted to enter the **Tag name** and, optionally, **Group▼**. Once done, click on **<Save>**.

⚙ **Gear icon** menu → TOOLS: Order cheques

TOOLS

The next group of available options under QBO is referred to as **TOOLS**. This is a list of features offered by QBO that are used occasionally and don't fall neatly into Lists. To access Tools, go to the ⚙ **Gear icon** and click on **Tools**.

Order cheques

Clicking on **Order cheques** will take you to a third-party service where you can order cheques for your business that are customized to QBO's specifications. These cheques can simply be put into your printer and QBO will automatically print the information from the cheque on to the page.

To set up cheques please refer to our section on Print Cheques.

Import data

If you are moving from another accounting software that is not QuickBooks Desktop or Sage Desktop (see import outside data below) then you can use this feature to import the following:

- Bank Data
- Customers
- Suppliers/vendors
- Chart of Accounts

- Products and Services
- Invoices
- Bills
- Journal Entries

Each option gives you a sample data file that demonstrates how the file must be formatted in order to import it. Once you have exported your data from your spreadsheet or other accounting software, you will then need to customize it to fit the formatting requirements and then save it as a csv (comma separated values) file. It is important that the formatting is exactly correct otherwise you will likely get an error message, or it will download incorrectly.

They also give you a recommendation to use a third-party app such *SAASAnt* which allows for more flexibility and a greater array of transaction types.

Import outside data

If you are using QBDT, the migration is fairly straightforward and can be done directly through QBO and QBDT without any third-party intervention as discussed in the section on Importing Your Data from Quickbooks Desktop.

If you are migrating from Sage desktop or Xero, you would download the guide, follow the instructions and send the data over to QBO support so that they can do the migration on your behalf.

Export data

If you want to export your key reports all from one place or you decide that you no longer want to use QBO either because you have ceased to be in business or you are transferring to another accounting software, you can use this feature to export the main reports that are required as a record of all your transactions. This is extremely important to have in case of audit or if you need to review details about a transaction in the future (even if you don't think you do). The reports downloaded are the following as of the dates that you select:

- General ledger
- Profit and loss
- Balance Sheet
- Trial balance

- Journal
- Customers
- Employees
- Suppliers

Additionally, there is an option to download key reports in XML format which can be used in case you are being audited by Revenue Canada.

Reconcile

A key feature of any accounting software is the ability to reconcile your bank and credit cards from the books to the actual statements. This is extremely important to ensure that you don't omit, duplicate or erroneously record any transactions and is an essential tool for discovering errors. This is discussed in the banking section.

Budgeting (Plus)

A budget is forecast of future revenues and Expenses. It is good practice, when you have a business, to create a budget to ensure that you are on track with your financial goals and to identify any cash flow or other issues that might arise. This is an advanced topic beyond the scope of this book.

Audit log

Historically accounting software was difficult to use by non-accountants because erroneous transactions could never simply be deleted. Instead, you had to reverse the transaction and re-enter it, which was tedious and seemingly unnecessary. The reason for this was to create an audit trail of each transaction so a user couldn't simply go in and delete or modify a transaction, which could result in fraud.

QuickBooks was somewhat revolutionary in that it allowed you to delete and modify transactions without having to re-enter them, to the chagrin of many accountants. To compensate for this, all versions of QBO have a detailed audit log that allows you to see every transaction that has been changed, entered, deleted, etc. and by which user. This is very helpful to review issues and errors and also to reconstruct transactions that may have been erroneously changed or deleted.

SmartLook

Clicking on this will give you a code that you can share with QBO support whenever you need help.

⚙️ **Gear icon** menu → **PROFILE: Feedback; Refer a friend**

PROFILE
_____

The final section on the ⚙️ **Gear icon** menu is for user-related functions and includes the following sections:

Feedback

Clicking on Feedback will open up a box where you can submit messages to QBO about anything relating to their product (and can be a useful outlet when frustrated). There is also an option to enclose a photo. This is simply a way to advise them of your thoughts and opinions but does not usually garner a response.

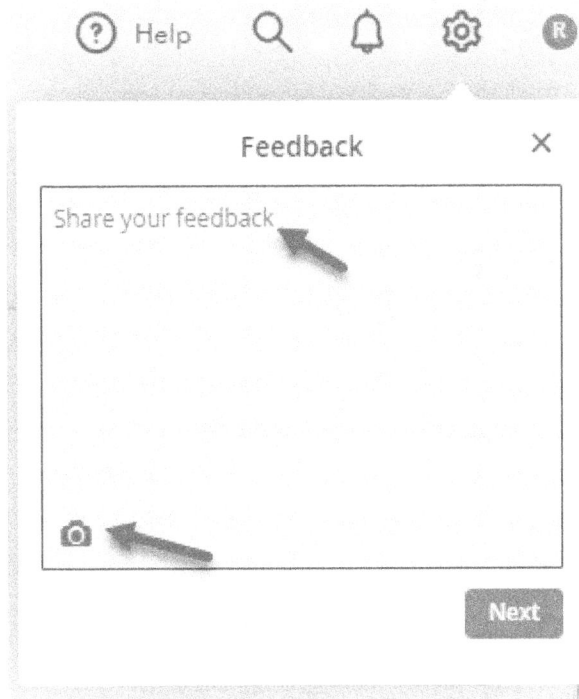

Refer a friend

This is a referral program offered by QBO where you receive a prepaid Visa card for a specific amount (currently $100) to anyone you refer who subscribes to QBO. In order to receive the referral bonus, the subscriber must use the referral link that you send to them through the sign-up form provided. The subscriber, by using this link, also receives a discount for a limited time.

Privacy

This takes you QBO's privacy policy, which is useful to read if you are concerned about how they are ensuring that your data is safe.

Switch company

QBO allows you to be a user on more than one subscription. If you are added as a user on another subscription, it will show up on this interface. You can then select the business that you want to access, click on **<Continue>,** and you will be redirected.

You can also sign out from this interface.

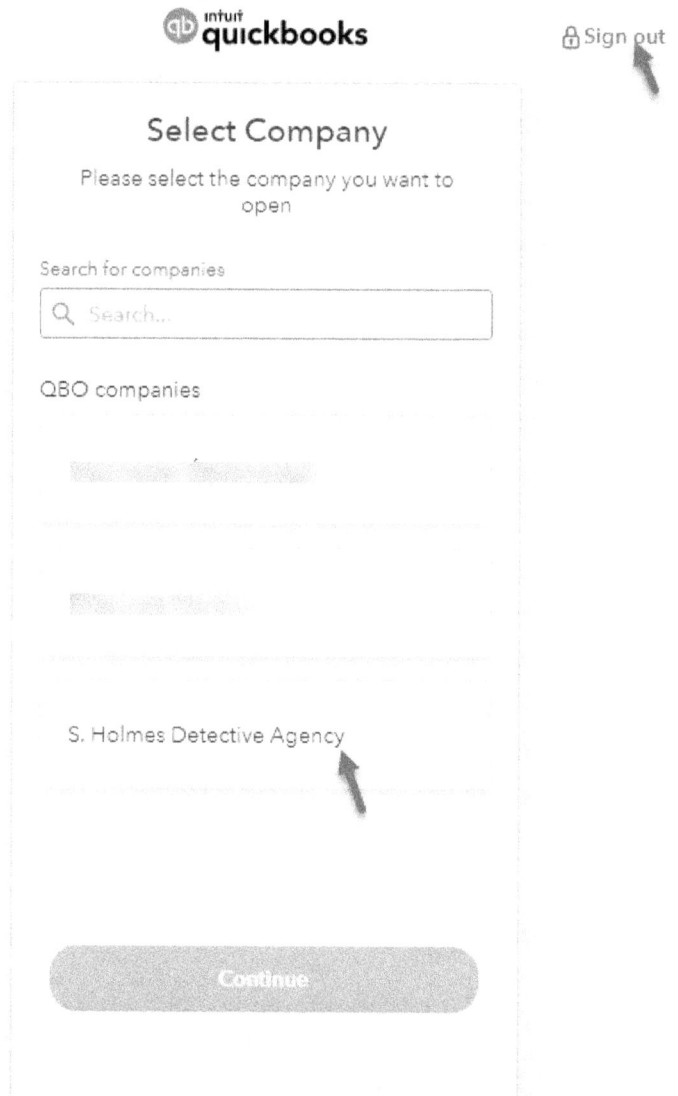

ADDITIONAL SETUP

Once you have customized your QBO file through the various options available in the ⚙ **Gear icon** menu, there are two additional steps to complete your setup:

1. Connect you bank and credit card accounts for automatic downloading of transactions.
2. Set up sales taxes (if applicable) so that you can assign sales taxes to transactions.

Connect Your Bank Accounts

One of my favourite features of QBO is the ability to connect your bank and credit card accounts. The advantages of linking your bank account include:

- Automatic downloading of transactions from your bank and credit card accounts on a daily basis.
- Significant reduction in data entry of individual transactions.
- Matching of invoice payments to Invoices.
- Matching of bill payments to Bills.
- Ability to create rules to categorize recurring transactions.
- Categorizing transactions and assigning sales tax codes directly from the downloaded transactions.
- Transferring payments between bank and credit card accounts.

> ➢ *Ideally, prior to setting up a new business you will have set up a business bank account and a credit card for your business. If you have an existing business, you will likely already have both. If you don't have business accounts, you can still connect them using the steps below, but you will have to be careful about and create a system for personal transactions.*

> ⇨ ***More on*** *why you should set up business bank and credit card accounts.*

How to Connect your Accounts

1. Hover on Transactions > (or Banking >)on the Left-hand Navigation Bar.
2. Click on **Banking** to open a new window.

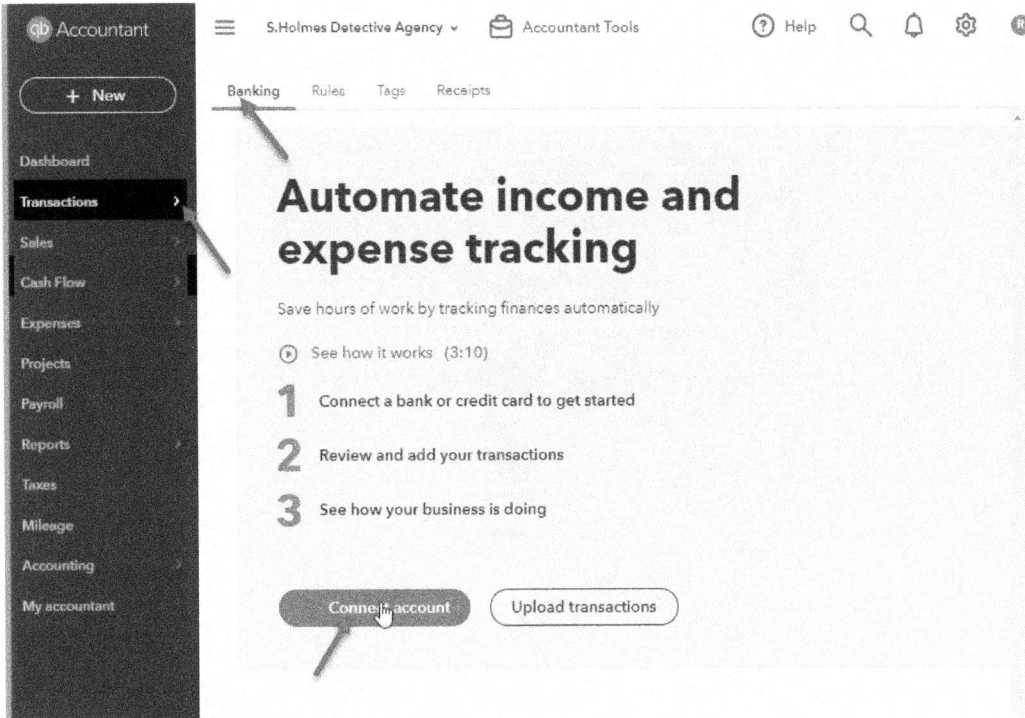

3.   Click <Connect account>.

Connect an account   ⑦ ✕

Let's get a picture of your profits

TD| ⊗

We support 20,000+ local and international banks.

TD Canada Trust - Easy ...   CIBC (Canadian Imperia...

Scotiabank (Canada)   Bank of Montreal (Cana...

American Express Credi...   Royal Bank of Canada

Paypal (Canada)   Vancity Credit Union (C...

(Show more)

4. Select your bank from the list or, if it doesn't appear on the list, click **<Show more>** or enter it into the **Search box**. QBO supports over 20,000 local and international banks so there is a good chance that it will be on the list.

5. Once you have selected your bank, enter your username and password. This will be the same username and password that you use to access your account online. If the information entered is incorrect, QBO will prompt you to try again. Once entered, click **<Continue>**.

Connect an account

Sign in to account

TD Canada Trust - Easy Web
http://www.tdcanadatrust.com/
1-866-222-3456

Username or Access Card

45123456789

Password

••••••••

SHOW

(Back)   (Continue)

At Intuit, the privacy and security of your information are top priorities.

Privacy

6. Usually, your bank will require some kind of security verification. There might be an option for text or email only or both. Select how you want to receive the security notification and click **<Continue>**.

Connect an account

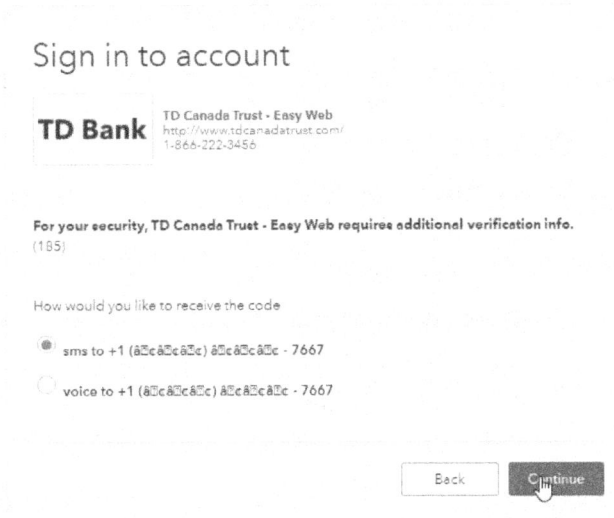

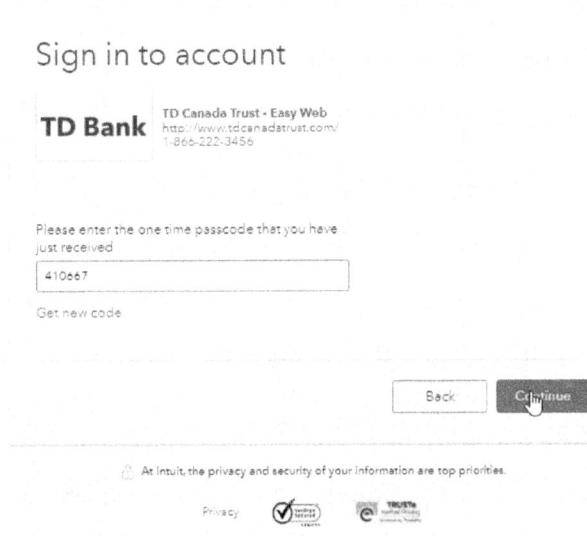

Sign in to account

TD Bank TD Canada Trust - Easy Web
http://www.tdcanadatrust.com/
1-866-222-3456

For your security, TD Canada Trust - Easy Web requires additional verification info. (185)

How would you like to receive the code

○ sms to +1 (ⓐⓒⓐⓒⓐⓒ) ⓐⓒⓐⓒⓐⓒ - 7667

○ voice to +1 (ⓐⓒⓐⓒⓐⓒ) ⓐⓒⓐⓒⓐⓒ - 7667

Back   Continue

🔒 At Intuit, the privacy and security of your information are top priorities.

Connect an account

7. Enter the code and click **<Continue>**.

Sign in to account

TD Bank TD Canada Trust - Easy Web
http://www.tdcanadatrust.com/
1-866-222-3456

Please enter the one time passcode that you have just received

410667

Get new code

Back   Continue

🔒 At Intuit, the privacy and security of your information are top priorities.

Privacy

8. The next screen shows you the existing bank accounts that are available using the online login.

9. Identify the bank accounts and credit cards that relate to your business and select the type of bank account from the dropdown, which will show you the bank and credit card accounts that you created when you were setting up your chart of accounts.

10. You also have the option to choose the date from which you want QBO to import the transactions:

Connect an account

TD CASH BACK VISA* CARD *8947
Balance $0.00

TD VISA

+ Add new

TD EVERY DAY CHEQUIN... *4935
Balance $35,467.05

TD Visa   Credit Card

We will pull transactions from the selected accounts from 01/01/2021. Or you can select a different date to pull transactions from. Some bank limitations may apply.

This year (01/01/2021)

Connect

Connect an account

Today (17/06/2021)

This month (01/06/2021)

This year (01/01/2021)   *6482   Checking

Last year (01/01/2020)

Custom...   cted accounts from 01/01/2021. Or you can select a
                               different date to pull transactions from. Some bank limitations may apply.

This year (01/01/2021)

Connect

If you are a brand-new business and this is a business bank/credit card account, you can choose a custom date range that goes back to the inception of the bank/credit card account.

If you are transitioning a business, then you should go back to the beginning of the current fiscal year for corporations, January 1st of the current year if you are a sole proprietor or the date from which you plan to start entering detailed transaction data.

> ➢ *Although there is flexibility in the transaction dates, every bank will only pull transactions going back to a certain date. So, even if you ask for the last two fiscal years, the bank might only provide the last three months of data.*

> ✓ *Your bank login might show all your business and personal bank accounts. In*
> *this case, you would only select the relevant business accounts.*

11. Assuming all goes well, you will see the next screens:

Connect an account

Connecting to TD Canada Trust - Easy Web...

At Intuit, the privacy and security of your information are top priorities.

Privacy

Connect an account   ⊘ ✕

All set! You're connected and ready to go.

12. You will automatically be taken to **[Banking]**, where you will see the accounts that you have added. We added two accounts – one credit card and one bank checking acount. All transactions for the selected date range for the credit card and then the bank account can be seen in the following screenshots:

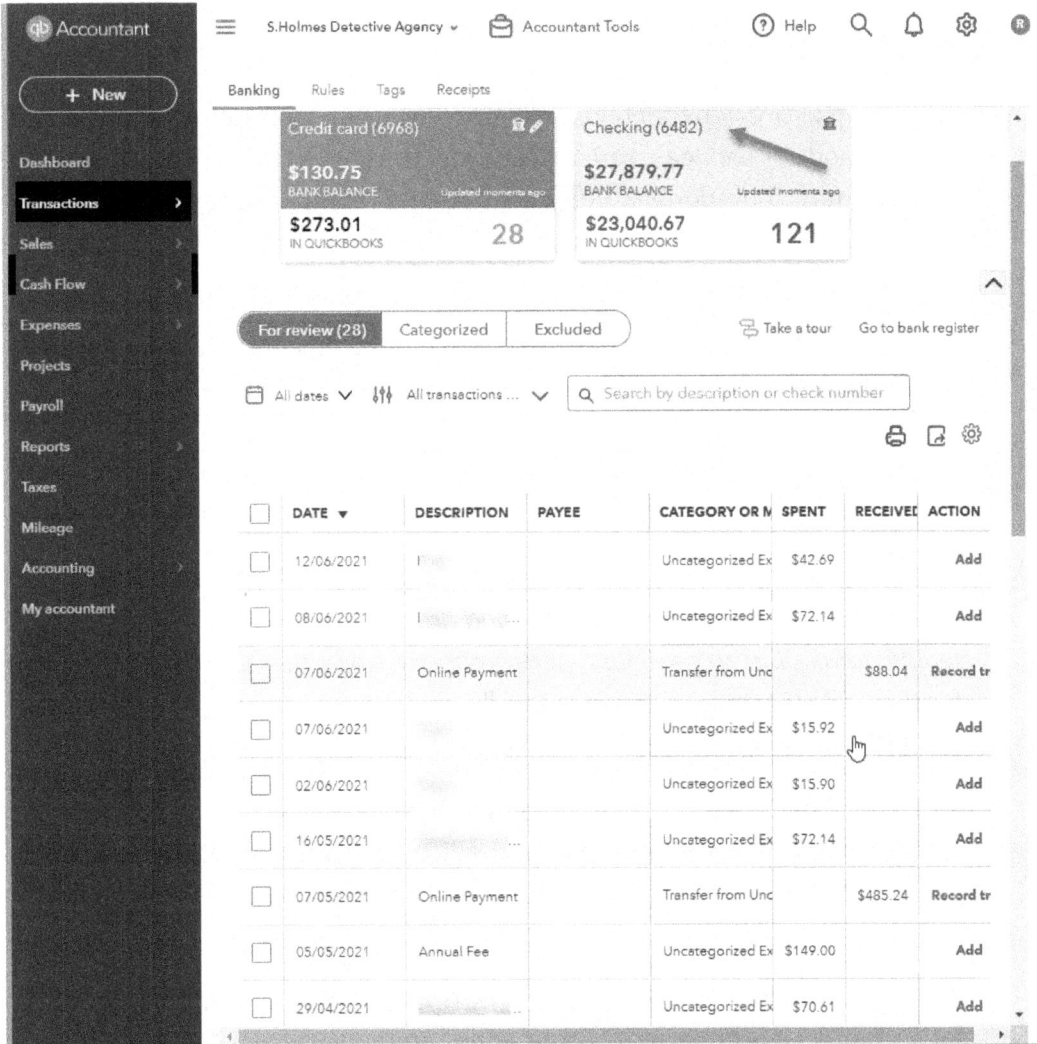

13. And that's it! You're done connecting your bank accounts.

> ➤ *Bank accounts can always be added at a later date using the same method.*

14. We will go over how to enter banking transactions in detail later.

Set Up Sales Taxes

Canadian businesses are generally required to register for sales taxes. This means that if you sell goods or services, you are required to charge GST/HST to other Canadian Customers. Additionally, you might also be required to sign up for QST or PST depending on the province in which your business is located or if you exceed a certain amount of sales to another province.

> ✓ *The upside of registering for sales tax is that you may also claim back 100% of the GST/HST paid on business related Expenses.*

Some businesses do not have to register for sales tax:

- If your total sales are $30,000 or less in the last four consecutive calendar quarters.

> ⚠ *Taxi operators, commercial ride-sharing drivers, and non-resident performers selling admissions to seminars, performances, and other events must register for the GST/HST, even if they are small Suppliers. i.e., they're sales are less $30,000 as defined above.*

- If you sell Exempt goods or services, which include long term residential rentals, medical/dental services (for medical purposes rather than cosmetic purposes), some child care and educational services, bank fees , insurance and many more.

- If you sell Zero Rated goods <u>exclusively</u>, then you are not required to register for GST/HST. It is however recommended to register anyway since even though you don't have to charge GST/HST, you can still claim back sales taxes paid on Expenses. Zero rated Expenses include basic groceries, prescription drugs, and sales of goods/services to Customers who do not reside in Canada. For example, if you sell your services to a client who is located in the US, then you do not have to charge them sales tax.

For a more detailed understanding of GST/HST please refer to the guidance from CRA.

> ➢ *If you have decided that you do not need to register your business for GST/HST, you can skip this step and come back to it later if you decide to register your business.*

Once you set up sales taxes in QBO, a field will appear on every transaction where you will have to enter a sales tax code.

How to Set Up Sales Tax

The process of setting up sales taxes is very simple.

1. On the QBO dashboard select **Taxes**from the **Left-hand Navigation Bar**. You will see the screen below:

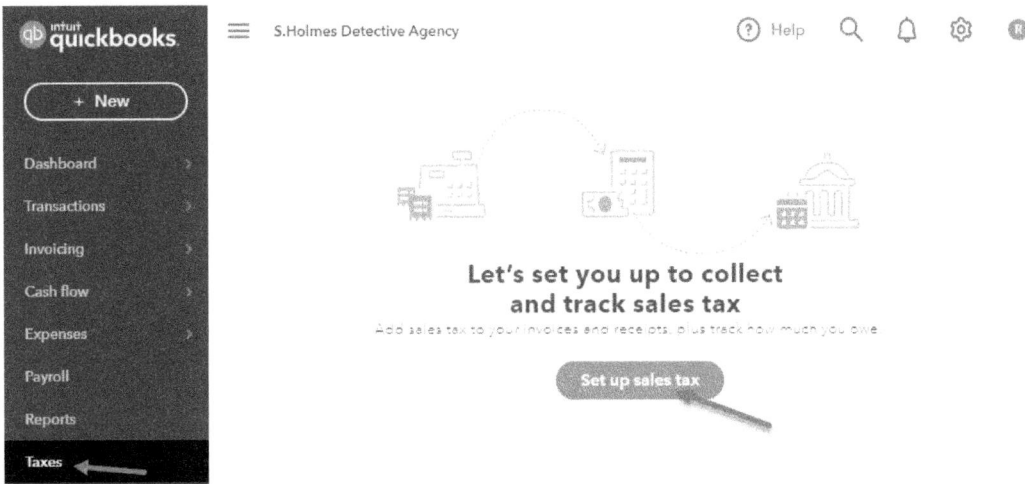

2. Click on <Set up sales tax>.

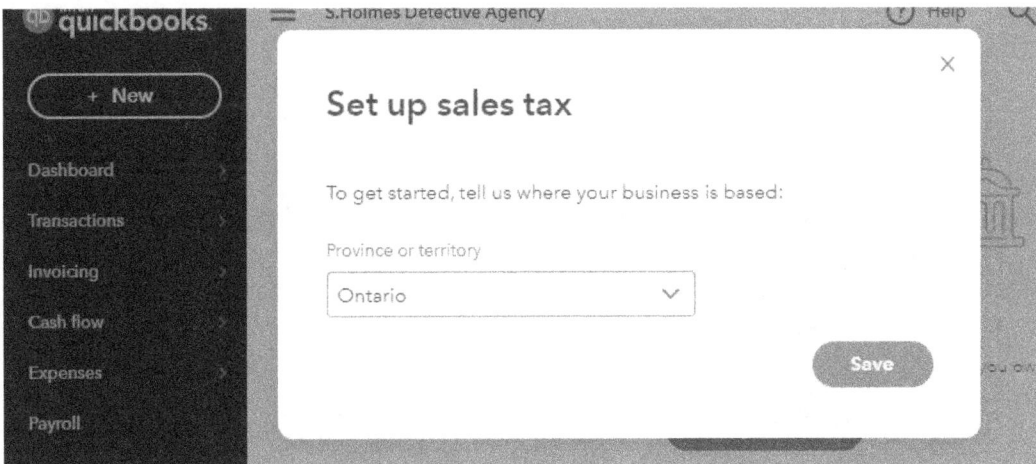

3. You will then be asked to select the province or territory where your business is located from a dropdown. For the purposes of our example, we will select Ontario.

4.   Click **<Save>,** which will take you to a new screen as follows:

Tell us how you currently handle this tax and we'll do the rest.

Agency
Canada Revenue Agency

Start of tax period

| January   ⌄ |

Filing frequency

| Yearly   ⌄ |

Reporting method

◉ Accrual

◯ Cash

GST/HST number

| ⬚⬚⬚⬚⬚⬚⬚⬚RT0001 | ⬚

(Next)

- **Agency** is automatically set to Canada Revenue Agency since Ontario is an HST jurisdiction.

> ➢   *If your business is registered for sales tax in Quebec, this will default to Revenue Quebec.*

- **Start of tax period ▾** is where you would select the month in which you registered for sales tax.
- **Filing frequency ▾** where you would select the frequency of sales tax reporting that you indicated when you registered. Choose Monthly, Quarterly, Half-yearly, or Yearly.

> ➤ *Every business that has registered for GST/HST has to file a sales tax return. The filing period can be monthly, quarterly, or annually. You can choose the frequency at which you file when you register for sales tax although there are specific thresholds at which a filing frequency is mandatory:*
> ⇨ *If your sales are $1.5 million or less you can file annually, quarterly, or monthly.*
> ⇨ *If your sales are over $1.5 million but less than $6 million, you can file quarterly or monthly.*
> ⇨ *If your sales exceed $6 million, you are required to file monthly.*

- **Reporting method** refers to accrual or cash . This will usually be the accrual method.
- **GST/HST number** is available from the letter confirming your business sales tax registration and usually ends with RT0001. This should be entered to ensure that it appears on your Invoices.

> ⚠ *It is mandatory for sales tax registrants to show their GST/HST number on their Invoices.*

5. Click on **<Next>** and you should see the following screen:

Now you can add sales tax to your transactions, and record your sales tax payments in QuickBooks.
Visit the sales tax page whenever you want to view your history, run reports, or track payments.

OK

6. Click on **<OK>**, and you will be taken to the sales tax interface which you will now see every time you click on **Taxes** from the **Left-hand Navigation Bar**.

You are now set up to charge sales tax to all Customers/clients who are based in Ontario.

How to Set Up Sales Tax for a Different Province

If you have Customers who are located in a province other than Ontario, you will likely have to charge them sales tax based on the province in which they are located. QBO makes it simple to add sales taxes for other provinces.

To add sales taxes for other provinces and to see other options available click on the **<Manage sales tax>** button from **Taxes** in the **Left-hand Navigation Bar**.

1. On the next screen you will see your existing settings including:

- Tax agency, which is Canada Revenue Agency (as noted above, if your business is in Quebec, this will show as Revenue Quebec).
- GST/HST number entered during setup.
- Three tax codes including HST Ontario at 13%, Exempt at 0%, and Zero Rated at 0% (discussed above).

To add tax for another province, click on **<Add tax>**:

NAME	TAX ON SALES	TAX ON PURCHASES	DESCRIPTION	ACTIONS
HST ON	13%	13%	Harmonized federal and provincial tax (Ontario)	Make inactive
Exempt	0%	0%	Tax-exempt	Make inactive
Zero-rated	0%	0%	Zero-rated	Make inactive

Manage sales tax

Tax agencies   Group rates

Show inactive   Add tax

Canada Revenue Agency
GST/HST
Filing: Yearly   GST/HST number: 826100992RT0001   + Add custom rate   Edit agency settings

1-3 of 3

2. This will bring up 3 options. The option that is applicable in this case is **Start tracking in a new province**. The other two options are very specific and not applicable to most Canadian businesses.

3. Clicking on **<Add>** will bring up a list of the provinces. Select the province where you expect to have customers from the dropdown:

4. Using Prince Edward Island (PEI) as our example, you will see a note that says "These taxes are added to GST/HST and are not separate taxes." This

means that taxes charged in PEI are part of the GST/HST regime and are remitted to CRA along with all other GST/HST collected. Click on **<Add>** in the bottom right hand corner.

5. You will see the new tax category created which reflects taxes at the PEI HST rate of 15%.

Manage sales tax   ⑦   ✕

Show inactive ⬤   Add tax

Tax agencies   Group rates

Canada Revenue Agency ✎
GST/HST

Filing: Yearly   GST/HST number: 826100992RT0001   + Add custom rate   ✎ Edit agency settings

NAME	TAX ON SALES	TAX ON PURCHASES	DESCRIPTION	ACTIONS
GST/QST QC - 9.975 ⌄	14.975%	14.975%	Combined federal and provincial tax (Quebe	Make inactive
GST	5%	5%	Federal goods and services tax	Make inactive
HST NS	15%	15%	Harmonized federal and provincial tax (Nova	Make inactive
HST ON	13%	13%	Harmonized federal and provincial tax (Ontar	Make inactive
Exempt	0%	0%	Tax-exempt	Make inactive
Zero-rated	0%	0%	Zero-rated	Make inactive
HST PE 2016	15%	15%	Combined federal and provincial tax (15% PE	Make inactive

Done

The tax codes noted above will be available as a dropdown for every transaction
that you enter in QBO going forward. You simply have to select the tax rate that is
applicable to the transaction. Click **<Done>** to leave this screen.

Print Cheques

Before you print cheques, QBO encourages you to print a sample cheque to ensure that your printer is set up correctly and you don't waste cheques.

To initiate the set up, click on **<+ New>** button on the top left-hand corner and select **Print cheques** from the **SUPPLIERS** column.

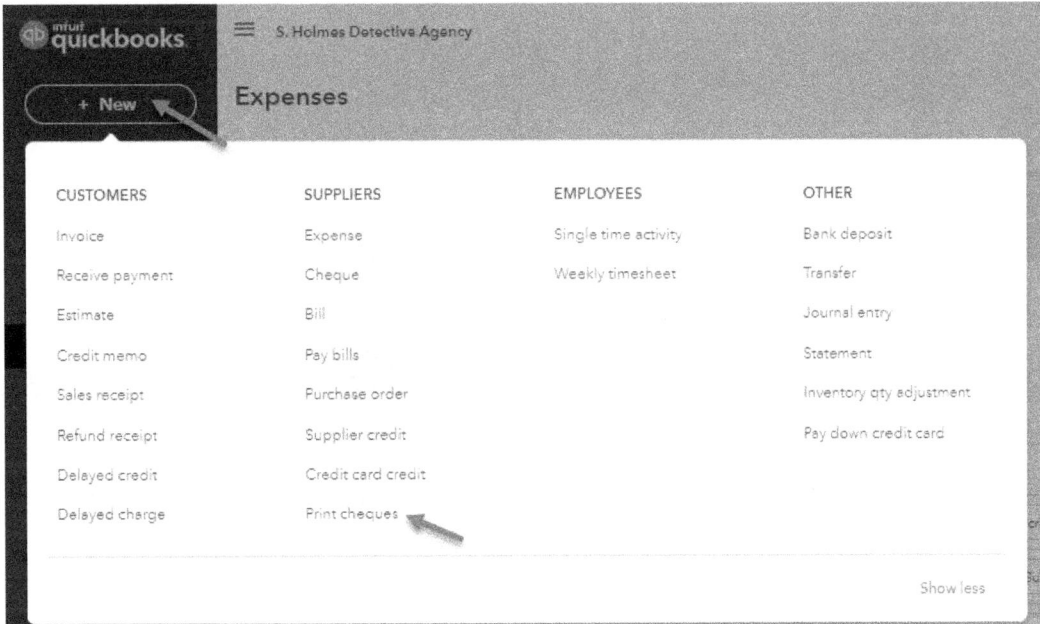

You will see the following screen with instructions:

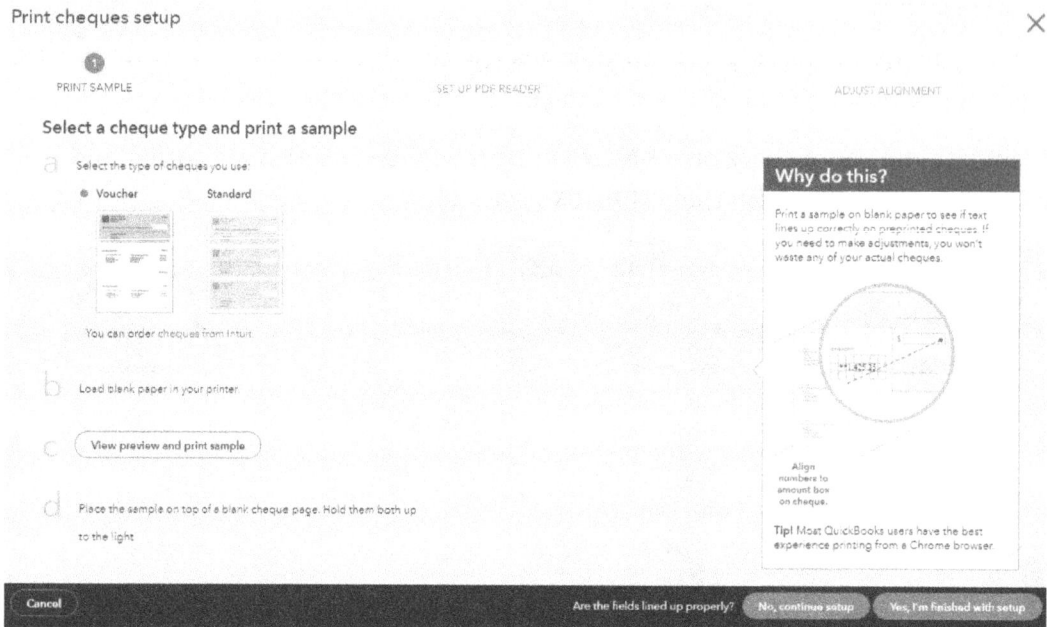

Follow the instructions to ensure that your cheque prints correctly.

Once everything looks ok, click on **<Yes, I'm finished with setup>**. You are now ready to print cheques, which we will discuss in greater detail in the Print Cheques section.

PART 3: QBO DAY-TO-DAY

CREATE CUSTOMERS AND INVOICES

A key feature in any accounting software is the ability to manage sales to Customers. QBO has significant functionality in this area.

On your dashboard you will see **Sales >** (or **Invoicing >** in some versions) on the **Left-hand Navigation Bar**. When you click on this, you will see the [**Overview**] dashboard below:

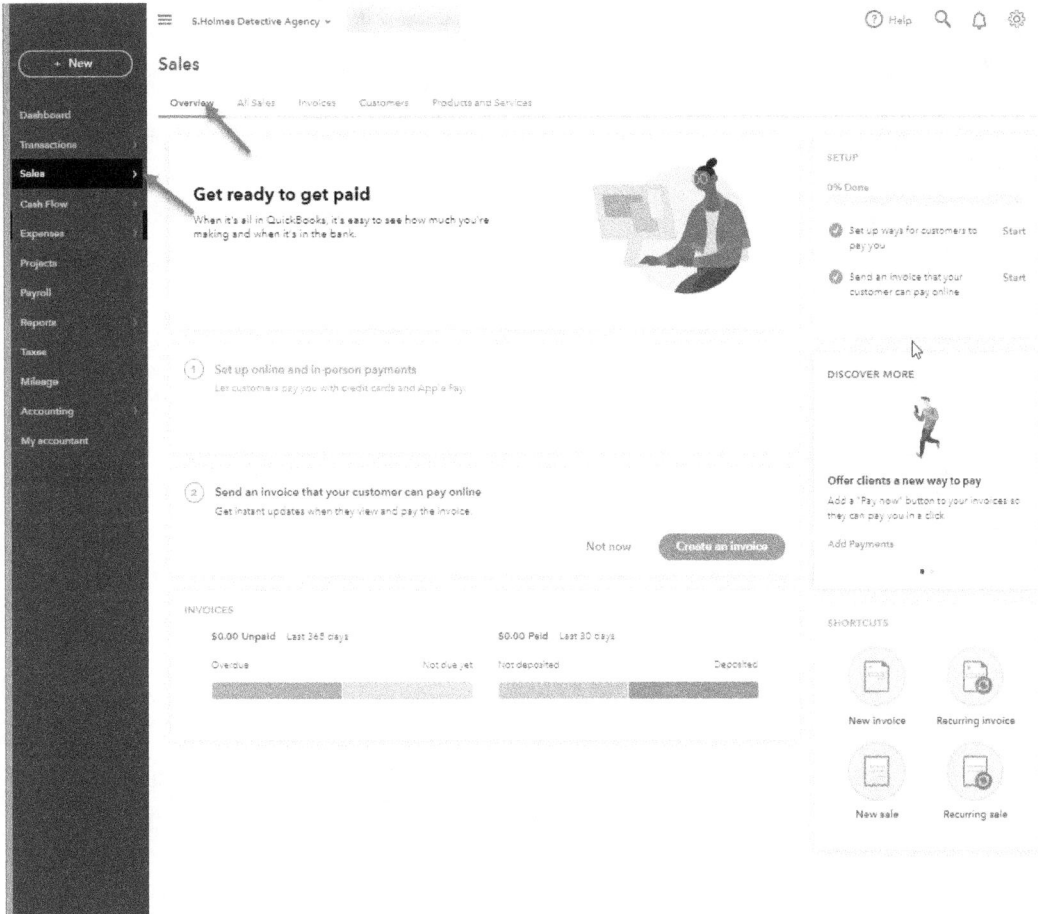

This dashboard gives you an overview of your sales, some shortcuts, and other options. Note the [**Overview**], [**All sales**], [**Invoices**], [**Customers**], and [**Products and Services**] tabs at the top.

Creating Customers

Let's create our first Customer:

1. Click on **[Customers]** at the top of the **Sales** dashboard.

2. Click on <Add customer manually>.

3. You will be presented with the customer information area where you can enter all pertinent details about your customer including:

Customer information

Title	First name	Middle name	Last name	Suffix	Email
Mr	Mike		Moriarty		moriarty@adversary.com

Company

Adversary Co.

Phone	Mobile	Fax
519-555-1234	519-555-1235	

* Display name as

Adversary Co.

Other	Website
	http://adversary.com

Print on cheque as ☑ Use display name

☐ Is sub-customer

Adversary Co.

Bill with parent ▼

Address | Notes | Tax info | Payment and billing | Language | Attachments | Additional Info

Billing address map		Shipping address map ☑ Same as billing address	
25 Westminister		25 Westminister	
London	Ontario	London	Ontario
N5V 0A4	Canada	N5V 0A4	Canada

Cancel   Privacy   Save

- **Title, First name, Middle name, Last name**, and **Suffix** allows you to be very precise in identifying individual customers/contact people.
- **Company** is for the business's registered name, if any.
- **Display name as** lets you decide how this customer will be shown in your internal navigation. This is a personal preference and can always be changed. Some of us like to see the name of the business while for others the first and last name of the individual customer or contact might be preferable.
- **Print on cheque** refers to the name that will be printed on the cheque. This is sometimes different from the name that you choose for the display name, e.g., if you choose the name of your customer rather than the name of their business for display purposes, you can use this section to set the actual name that appears on the cheque.
- **Email** and **Phone, Mobile**, and **Fax** numbers.
- **Other** for any contact method or information not covered above, and **Website**.

- **Is sub-customer** is an option that can be used when you have a number of Customers that fall under one master Customer. For example, you might invoice a single chain store, but you might ship your product to various individual stores in different Locations.
- **[Address]** is the first of several tabs at the bottom.
- **Billing address** and **Shipping address** if this is different from the billing address.
- **[Notes]** is next. You can enter information about the client that is pertinent to either you or to your staff.

Customer information   ✕

| Address | Notes | Tax info | Payment and billing | Language | Attachments | Custom fields | Additional Info |

Notes

Check to make sure that no evil plan is involved

(Cancel)   Privacy   (Save)

- **[Tax info]** allows you to enter the customer GST/HST number in **Tax Reg. No.** for information purposes. You can also check ☑**Assign default tax code** to set up a **Default tax code ▼** for the default sales tax rate that you charge the customer. This rate will then automatically populate when you create an Invoice for this specific customer, so that you don't have to look it up each time.

Customer information   ✕

| Address | Notes | Tax info | Payment and billing | Language | Attachments | Custom fields | Additional Info |

Tax Reg. No.   ☑ Assign default tax code
                                          Default tax code

                                          HST ON   ▼

(Cancel)   Privacy   (Save)

- **[Payment and billing]** is where you enter details about how you generally
  collect payment from this customer, which will also prepopulate upon
  creation of an Invoice.

Customer information   ✕

| Address | Notes | Tax info | Payment and billing | Language | Attachments | Custom fields | Additional Info |

Preferred payment method

Cheque ▼

Preferred delivery method

Print later ▼

Terms

Due on Receipt ▼

Opening balance   as of

| 30/06/2021

Cancel   Privacy   Save

- **Preferred payment method ▼** lets you set the payment type set up as
  discussed in the Payment Methods section
- **Preferred delivery method ▼** allows you to indicate whether you would like
  to print the Invoice later or email the Invoice to the customer.
- **Terms ▼** represent the amount of time after which the Invoice is issued that
  payment is due. See our chapter on Terms.
- **Opening balance** is used to enter any carryforward balances for the
  customer if you are moving from another accounting software. I
  recommend that opening balances be entered as a Journal Entry rather than
  entering anything here.

- **[Language]** is your preferred language for each customer. QBO has several options to **Send invoices to this customer in ▼**.

Customer information   ×

| Address | Notes | Tax info | Payment and billing | Language | Attachments | Additional Info |

Send invoices to this customer in

English ▼

English

French

Spanish

Italian

Chinese (traditional)

Portuguese (Brazil)

Cancel   Make inactive   Privacy   Save

- **[Attachments]** allows you to attach documents such as agreements, contracts, or special instructions directly to customer for easy retrieval and review.
- **[Additional Info]** (PLUS) is where you can create different customer types. This is an advanced topic and beyond the scope of this book.

✓   *Not all boxes in the Customer set up have to be filled. You can choose to only enter what is relevant and edit in the future if needed.*

4.   Click on **<Save>** to go back to the customer interface.

5.   Here you can see a list of all your existing Customers:

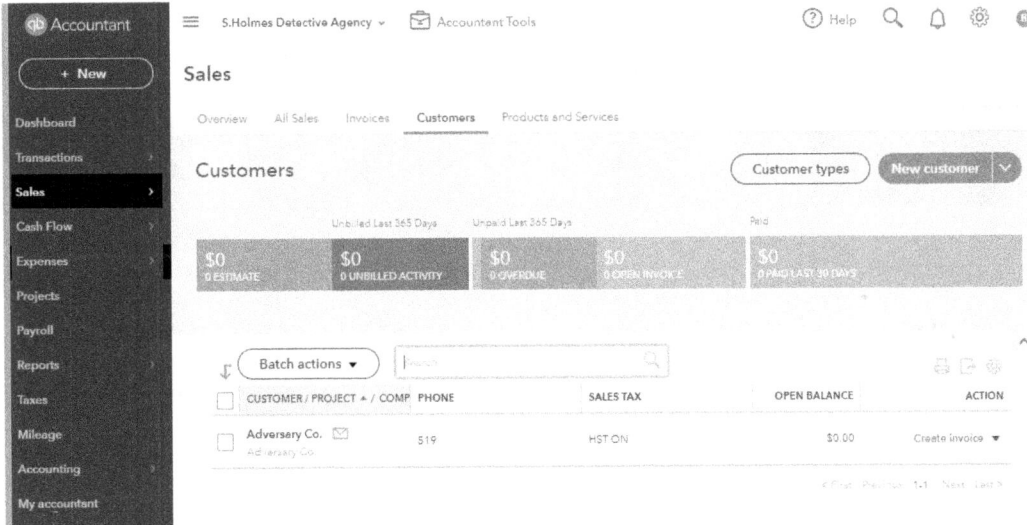

> ➤ *Note that new Customers will now be created by clicking on* **<New customer▼>** *on the top right-hand side of this interface. Follow the same procedure outlined above.*

Creating Invoices

An Invoice is a transaction record that is given to a Customer that lists the products or services that you have provided and the amount that the Customer owes you.

There are various components of an Invoice that we will discuss below:

An invoice can be created in one of two ways in QBO:

Go to **Sales >** (or **Invoicing >**) from the **Left-hand Navigation Bar** of the dashboard and click on **[Invoices]**.

Click on **<+ New>** button from the **Left-hand Navigation Bar** of the QBO interface
and select **Invoice** under **CUSTOMERS**.

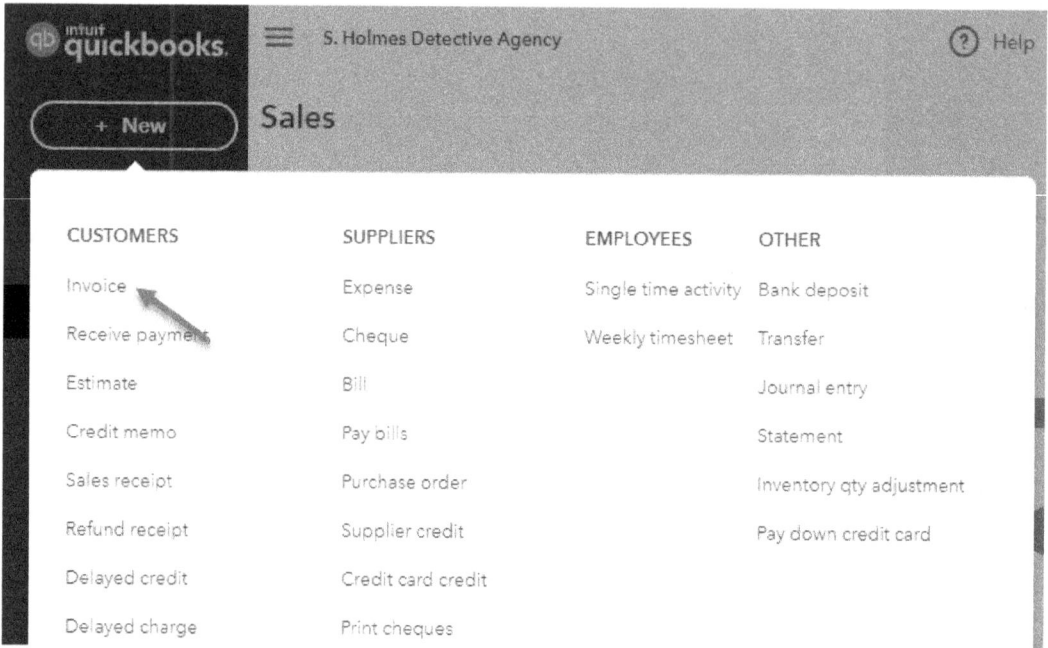

Below is an example of a completed invoice:

Let's examine each field:

1. Customer Information

- **Customer ▼ :** You will be prompted to enter a customer for which a dropdown is provided. You can select the customer from the dropdown OR if you have many customers, you can simply start typing the name of the customer and QBO will narrow down the field. After entering the details, you will note that the following fields prepopulate with the details that were entered when we set up the customer above:

- Customer email.
- Billing address.
- Shipping to.

- Terms ▼.
- **Invoice date** is simply today's date and can be changed.
- **Due date** is calculated from the invoice date by adding the number of days indicated in the terms e.g., in this case the invoice date and due date are the same since we put 0 days and payment upon receipt when we entered the terms for this customer.

> ➢ *If these fields were not entered when you set up the customer, you can add them directly in the Invoice. Note that they will not update the customer info and as such it is better to update the customer directly.*

The following fields are indicated if you choose to turn on **Shipping** in the sales form content section of the [Sales] tab.

- **Ship via** lets you put in a shipping method.
- **Shipping date** is the date a product is shipped.
- **Tracking no.** allows you to enter tracking info for the shipped item(s).

> ✓ *You can also create a customer directly from the Invoice interface in Customer ▼ by selecting +Add New. You would then enter the name of the customer and click <Save>. If you use this method of adding a customer, you can go back to your customer page and edit the details at a later time.*

Invoice no.304090

Customer ⑦

| Select a customer | ⌄ |

\+ Add new

Adversary Co.   Customer

Amazon   Customer

Customer email ⑦   Cc/Bcc

| Separate emails with a comma |

☐ Send later ⑦

🕐 **Invoice no.304090**

Customer ⑦   Customer email ⑦   Cc/Bcc

[Select a customer   ⌄]   [Separate emails with a comma   ]

New Customer   ⑦

* Name

[|]

+ Details   (Save)

                                                                  Due date

─────────────────────────────────   [25/08/2021   ]

        (Import your Gmail contacts)

2. The **Invoice no.** can be automatically assigned or entered directly. This is also discussed in sales form set up. The advantage of an automated invoice numbering system is that every invoice number in a series is accounted for and you don't have to take the extra time to choose and assign a number.

3. **Location ▼** (PLUS) is another classification type. This is an advanced topic and outside of the scope of this book.

4. **Tags**, as discussed in the section on tags, are also a classification type that is more granular and allows you to create reports for everything with the same tag.

5. **Payment method ▼** , **Reference no.**, and **Deposit to ▼** indicates how the customer will be paying, an additional reference number if applicable, and the bank account to which the deposit (see point 13 below) has been deposited. This will only appear if you have turned on **Deposit** in the section on Sales Form Content.

6. **SERVICE DATE** can be used if there was a specific date on which the services were provided that is different from the invoice date. This is often used by

trades and will also only appear if turned on in the section on Sales Form
Content found in the Account and settings tab.

7. **PRODUCT/SERVICE** is the type of product or service that is being provided
    and can be set up by going to the Products and services section or it can be
    set up by entering the name of the product or service directly, which will
    bring up the same window as discussed earlier, and entering the pertinent
    details. The **DESCRIPTION** represents the details of the product or service
    being provided which can be customized here or entered when setting up
    the product/service, in which case this field will pre-populate.

8. **QTY**, **RATE**, and **AMOUNT** refer to the number of hours or units, the rate for
    each unit, and the total amount that is derived by multiplying **QTY** by **RATE**.

9. **SALES TAX** is the GST/HST and provincial rates, if applicable, and is
    represented by a code as discussed in the setting up sales tax section. This is
    either pre-populated if entered in the customer details when setting up the
    customer or can be entered directly by selecting a code from the dropdown.

10. **CLASS** is a classification similar to location. This is an advanced topic and
    beyond the scope of this book.

11. **Message on invoice** can be customized here. You might state how to make
    payment or make other comments about the Invoice that are not in the
    description section. This can also be set up in the sales form section if you
    have the same message going out to all your Customers. If you do set it up
    in settings, it can always be edited here as well.

12. **Discount percent ▼** appears when turned on in the Sales Form Content
    found in the Account and settings section. If you regularly give your
    Customers discounts, you would leave it on. If not, it might make sense to
    turn it off.

    The **Shipping ▼** dropdown, similar to discounts, is useful if you charge
    extra shipping to your clients. In this case the dropdown asks which tax
    code applies to shipping. This is usually the same tax code as the Invoice as
    shipping is taxable in Canada.

> ✓ *You can also set up a discount as a separate service and it would simply be
> reflected as a line item on the Invoice. To create a new service, please refer
> to the Product and services section.*

13. **Deposit** is where you would enter any down payments or retainers paid on the Invoice prior to full payment.
14. **Balance due** is what the customer owes and includes the net amount plus sales tax less any discounts and deposits.
15. 📎 **Attachments** allows you to attach any pertinent documents such as purchase orders from Customers, sales order, or an agreement.
16. The bottom of the Invoice has a **Bottom Bar**, which allows you perform a number of tasks:

- **<Cancel>** the Invoice.
- **Print or Preview** which is useful if you want to see what the Invoice will look like to the customer.
- **Make recurring** allows you to set up a recurring invoice at certain intervals discussed in our chapter on recurring transactions.
- **Customize** allows you to change the format of the Invoice.
- **More** has several dropdown options and only appears after you have saved the Invoice.
- **Copy** allows you to copy an Invoice. This is particularly useful when you would like to create a similar invoice with a couple of minor changes. When you click on **Copy**, an identical invoice is created where you can edit any of the fields and then resave it as a new invoice. The one field that you do have to change when you copy an Invoice is the invoice number since it is a brand-new Invoice.
- **Void** allows you to nullify an Invoice while maintaining it in your history of Invoices. The invoice number and other details will be preserved while the invoice amount will be changed to $0.00.
- **Delete** simply allows you to delete the whole invoice. If you have made an error, it might make more sense to delete rather than voiding.

- **Transaction journal** brings up the accounting entry (for those of you who enjoy some behind the scenes technical details). The journal allows you to see which accounts, in your Chart of Accounts, are impacted by this transaction. See the following:

You will note that **Accounts Receivable (A/R)** is debited, which means that there is an increase in A/R since *Adversary Co.* owes you money.

Sales are credited, which means that there is an increase in sales.

GST/HST Payable is credited, which means an increase in the liability. This amount is payable to the government.

Discounts given are a reduction in the sale amount and as such are debited.

Checking (6482) receives a deposit that increases the cash balance and is therefore debited.

- **Audit history** allows you to see exactly when the Invoice was entered and every time you or another user has made changes to this specific invoice.

17. Once you have entered everything and are satisfied that the Invoice looks ok, you have several choices:

Subtotal	$1,160.00
Discount percent ▼ 10	-$116.00
Shipping Select Shipping tax ▼	
	135.72
HST (ON) @ 13% on 1,044.00	
Total	$1,179.72
Deposit	500.00
Balance due	$679.72

Save and new

Save and close

Save and send

Save   **Save and share link** ▼

- **<Save>** the Invoice which simply saves the Invoice without changing windows.
- Clicking the down arrow on **<Save and share link| ▼ >** opens up additional options in a dropdown.
- Save and new takes you to the next blank invoice and is useful if you are doing more than one invoice at a time.
- Save and close exits you out of the Invoice and takes you back to the previous interface.
- Save and send takes you to another screen where you can then email the Invoice to your client. You will see in the screenshot below that it automatically creates an email with a summary of the Invoice and a PDF attachment. It also prepopulates an email message, which can be set up in Messages found in the Sales Tab section and changed here. Finally, there is

an option to select credit cards as a payment option if you are signed up for QBO payments as discussed in the section on payments. If you do select this option, the Invoice will include a link in the email that will allow your customer to pay directly by credit card.

- **<Save and share link▼ >** if you would rather simply send a link to the Invoice to your customer manually, you would select this option which will bring up a clickable link for you to copy and paste.

Receiving Payments

After you have sent your Invoice to your Customer, the corresponding Payment of the Invoice has to be recorded in QBO. There are four ways that you can "receive payment" to close out an Invoice in QBO.

1. **QBO Credit Card Payments**: If you are signed up for credit card payments with QBO, the allocation of the payment will be done automatically by QBO. It is important to make sure that the correct bank account is selected when setting up the payments.

2. **Match from Banking Download**: If you have set up your banking transactions to download automatically, and the amount of the payment deposited into your bank account EXACTLY matches the amount of the Invoice, you will usually see a green highlighted **1 record found** notification in QBO and the option to match it. In this case, you would review the details in the banking transaction to make sure that the payment is in fact for the Invoice to which it is matched. If so, you would click on **Match** and the payment is then automatically entered.

> ➤ *You will note here that since there are two payments for the same amount, they are both matching to the same invoice. Once you have clicked on* **Match** *for the correct payment, the second match option will disappear.*

3. **Manually Find Match**: Click any where on the payment.

⚠ *Do not click on Add.*

The payment expands to show details and other options:

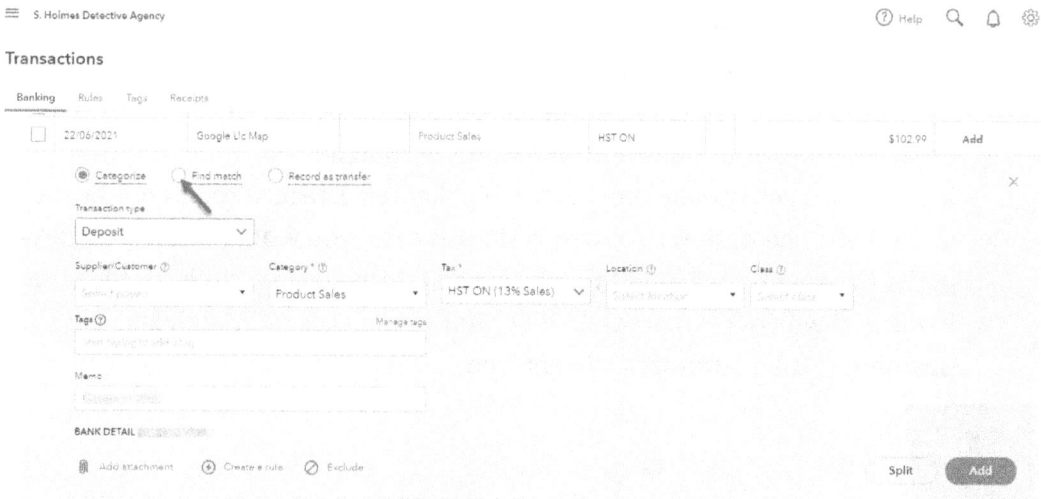

Click on ⊙ **Find Match**.

A new window opens up which lists Invoices for which payments have not yet been received (also referred to as "Outstanding Invoices" in accounting terminology).

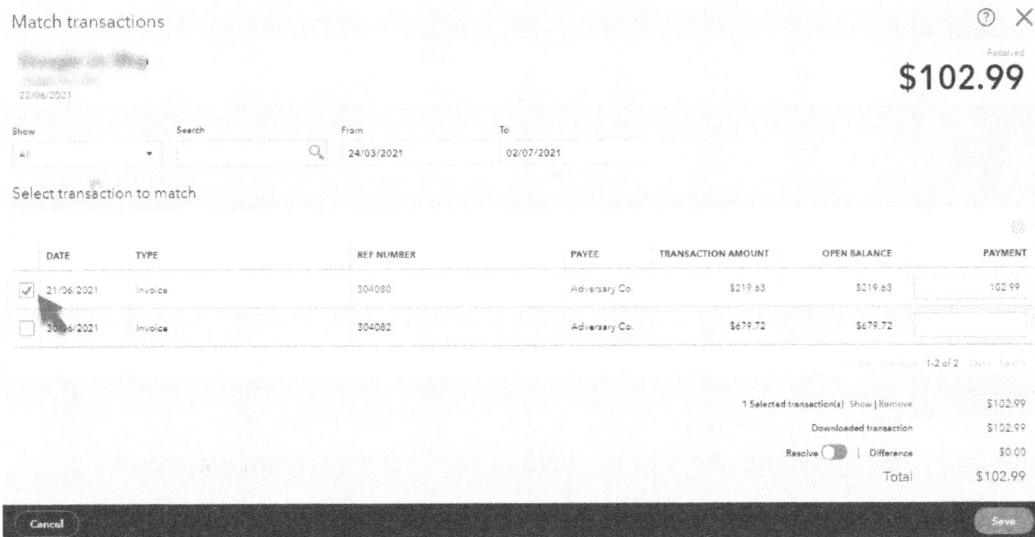

Click on the ☑ **checkbox** to the left of the date to select the Invoice to which the payment relates.

The payment of $102.99 is automatically allocated to the Invoice of $219.63. This represents a partial payment. In QBO, once this payment is allocated, it will show a balance remaining for this invoice of $219.63 - $102.99 = $116.64.

Click on **<Save>** at the bottom right to enter the transaction and exit out back to the banking transactions screen.

> ✓ *This also works when you have one deposit for payments from multiple Customers.*

> ✓ *At the top of the **Match transactions** screen there is an area where you can enter the **From** and **To** dates of the Invoices to search. If your invoice does not appear and you know that it is outstanding, it is likely that the date range needs to be expanded.*

4. **Enter payment manually**: If you are not downloading the banking transactions, you can also add the payment manually. To add a payment:

Go to **Sales >** (or **Invoicing >**) on the **Left-hand Navigation Bar** and click on **[Invoices]**.

You will see a list of unpaid Invoices that have **Receive payment** as an **ACTION** item.

Click on **Receive payment** next to the Invoice for which payment was received.

This will take you to a prepopulated **Receive payment** form:

- **Customer** represents the customer on which you clicked.
- **Email** is their email address which is entered through the customer details.
- **Payment date** represents the date on which the actual payment was received. This usually defaults to today's date. If the payment was received on a different date, then this should be edited to reflect the date the payment was deposited into the bank account.
- **Payment method ▼** represents how the payment was made, such as cheque or credit card. If the payment method is not available in the dropdown, you can add it directly in this screen by clicking on **add new**.
- **Reference no** is usually available on the payment notification from the customer. This can also be left blank.
- **Deposit to** is the account in which the payment is deposited. This could be your primary bank account or another account such as Paypal or Stripe.
- **Amount received** represents the amount of the payment which defaults to the remaining balance owing on the Invoice that you selected. If the payment amount is different, you would change it here to match the payment amount.
- **Outstanding transactions** list all the Invoices that have not yet been paid for this customer. The invoice that you selected for receiving payment will automatically be checked, however, if you received payment for more than one invoice you can also check the additional Invoices.
- **Credits** list all of the credit memos (discussed in our section on credit memos) or overpayments and can be offset against payment received. To reduce the payment received by the credit memo simply click on the **checkbox** next to the credit memo that you want to apply against the payment.
- **Due date** shows the date by which the Invoice is supposed to be paid
- **Original** amount represents the full amount of the Invoice
- **Open balance** is the full amount of the Invoices less any payments that have already been applied
- **Payment** is the amount received from the customer against that specific invoice.

> ✓ *When you have multiple Invoices and credits the Customer should provide you with a statement that breaks down all the payments and Invoices so that you reconcile their statement to your records.*

- **Amount to apply** represents the total of the payment received less any credits.
- **Amount to credit** are any overpayments that will be applied to a future invoice and will show up as a credit under the credit section
- **Memo** allows you to enter any pertinent notes relating to the payment
- **Attachments** such as the payment statement or notification can be uploaded here
- **<Save and new| ▼ >** allows you to enter a new payment. Clicking the down arrow will open a dropdown menu:
- Save and close will record the transactions and exit back to the main interface.

Other Types of Sales Transactions

In addition to creating Invoices and receiving payments, QBO has several other sales-related transactions. These are discussed in detail in this section.

To access the other types of sales transactions, go to **Sales >** (or **Invoicing >**) on the **Left-hand Navigation Bar** and then **[All Sales]**. Click on **<New transaction>** to access the dropdown that lists each type.

> ⇵ *You can also access the dropdown by going directly to the customer as explained below.*

Estimates

An estimate, as the name suggests, allows you to create a proposal in QBO to submit to your customer. It is a non-posting transaction, which means that it does not affect any of your numbers until it is converted into an Invoice. Once the estimate is accepted, it can easily be converted into an Invoice.

To enter an estimate, go to **Sales >** (or **Invoicing >**) on the **Left-hand Navigation Bar** and then **[Customers]**. Select the customer for whom you want to enter the Estimate and click on Estimate in the dropdown for **<New transaction▼ >**.

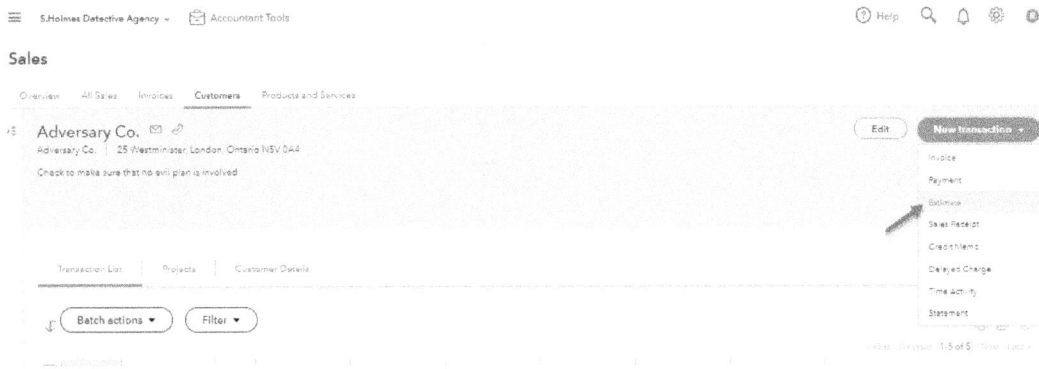

> ↻ *Alternatively, click **<+ New>** and click on **Estimate** which can be found under* **CUSTOMERS**.

The fields on the estimate are identical to a sales invoice with a few exceptions:

- **Estimate status ▼** is a dropdown that lets you indicate whether the estimate is:
- **Pending** for when you are waiting to hear back from your customer.
- **Accepted** for when the customer accepts the estimate.
- **Closed** meaning that the estimate has already been fully invoiced.
- **Rejected** for when the customer does not accept the estimate.
- **Estimate date** is where you enter the date of the estimate. This can be important if estimates are valid only for a certain number of days.
- **Estimate no.** follows a different number series than invoicing and can be entered manually or will be automatically entered by QBO.

Once you have saved the estimate, a new button, **<Create invoice| ▼ >** on the top right, will show on the estimate that then allows you to create an Invoice directly

If you want to go ahead and **<Create invoice| ▼ >**, it will bring up another box that
gives you some options on **How much do you want to invoice?**:

- **Total of all estimate lines** simply allows you to invoice for the full amount of
  the estimate.
- ☐ **%** **of each line** = allows you to choose a fixed percentage to apply to all
  lines.
- **Custom amount for each line** lets you select an individual amount for each
  line on the estimate that you want to invoice.

For our purposes, I have chosen to customize the amount for each line. Click
<Create invoice>.

A new Invoice, based on the Estimate, is generated:

You will note that the **Estimate date** and **Estimate no.** now convert to **Invoice date** and **Invoice no.** automatically. You can also click on the original estimate by going to **1 linked Estimate** on the top left. The bottom right also shows you details of the estimate.

Additionally, there is a new field, **DUE**, **that** allows you to enter the amount or percentage of the estimate that you will be invoicing at the present. An invoice will be created which you would then save and can be sent to the customer.

When you go back to the dashboard for the same customer you will note that the estimate and the Invoice that you have just created appear in the history for the customer:

DATE	TYPE ▲	NO.	MEMO	DUE DATE	TOTAL BEFORE SALES TAX	SALES TAX	TOTAL	STATUS	ACTION
11/08/2021	Estimate	1002		11/08/2021	$1,250.00	$162.50	$1,412.50	Pending	Create invoice ▾
05/07/2021	Estimate	1001		05/07/2021	$1,250.00	$162.50	$1,412.50	Closed	Print ▾
05/07/2021	Charge	1		05/07/2021	$50.00	$6.50	$56.50	Closed	
05/07/2021	Time Charge			05/07/2021	$250.00	$0.00	$250.00	Open	Create invoice
26/07/2021	Invoice	304088		26/07/2021	$1,250.00	$162.50	$1,412.50	Overdue	Receive payment ▾

S. Holmes Detective Agency

Sales

Overview   All Sales   Invoices   **Customers**   Products and services

Adversary Co. ✉ 🔗

Adversary Co.   25 Westminister, London, Ontario N5V 0A4

Check to make sure that no evil plan is involved

New transaction ▾

$2,293.61 OPEN

$2,350.11 OVERDUE

Transaction List   Projects   Customer Details

Batch actions ▾   Filter ▾

Also, next to the Estimate is an **ACTION** that allows you **Create invoice▾**, which will take you through the same process of creating an Invoice from an Estimate. You can continue to invoice the customer a percentage, a fixed amount, or the balance of the estimate once the work is completed.

> ➤ *QBO, unlike the desktop version, does not currently have the ability to create sales orders. However, Estimates offer very similar functionality to sales orders and can be used instead.*

Sales Receipt

There are certain types of businesses such as retail or tradespeople that receive cash upon receipt or delivery of the product, or the service is provided at the same time as the payment is received. In these cases, rather than creating a separate invoice and payment, you would issue a sales receipt that combines both actions into one transaction.

Like with Estimates, you can go directly to the Customer from **Sales >** (or **Invoicing >**) on the **Left-hand Navigation Bar** and then **[Customers]**. Select your Customer, and when the new window opens, click on **Sales Receipt** from the **<New transaction▼>** dropdown.

> ⤻ *Alternatively, click **<+ New>** and click on **Sales receipt** which can be found under **CUSTOMERS**.*

You will note that a sales receipt looks very similar to an Invoice and also follows the automatic numbering assigned to Invoices. The primary difference, as mentioned above, is that you do not have to record a payment for a sales receipt as this is all part of one transaction.

> ❖ *In our case, Mr. Moriarty has paid SHDA up front for photos of his dog and demanded a receipt as he is very meticulous with his records.*

Other differences include:

- **Sales Receipt date** instead of Invoice date.
- No **Due date** nor **terms**, since invoicing and payment effectively happen concurrently.
- **Sales receipt no.** instead of Invoice no.

- **Payment method** is an additional field on a Sales Receipt since payment is received at the time of issuing the receipt.
- **Reference no.** can be the cheque number or other identifier relating to the payment or it can be left blank.
- **Deposit to▼** references the bank account in which the payment was received.

Credit Memo

A Credit Memo is effectively the opposite of an Invoice. It is a credit that is given to a customer and either reduces the amount of the Invoice that they currently owe or can be applied against future Invoices. To create a Credit Memo, click **Sales >** (or **Invoicing >**) on the **Left-hand Navigation Bar** and then **[Customers]**. Select your Customer, and when the new window opens, click **<New transaction▼>** and then Credit Memo from the dropdown.

> ☝ *Alternatively, click* **<+ New>** *and click on* **Credit memo** *which can be found under* **CUSTOMERS**.

The format of a Credit Memo is almost identical to an Invoice, with a few small exceptions, and like Sales Receipts also follows Invoice numbering. Below is an example of a Credit Memo:

- **Credit Memo Date** replaces Terms, Invoice Date, and Due Date on an Invoice, which are not applicable for a Credit Memo.

When a Credit Memo is entered, the balance owing from the customer is reduced or, if there is no balance owing, the amount receivable from the customer becomes a negative. This means that you actually owe money to the customer as a consequence of the credit memo.

As discussed in the receive payments section, the Credit Memo will appear when you are creating a Payment and can be checked to automatically reduce a payment received.

Delayed Charge

A Delayed Charge is similar to a reminder that once set up will show up on the customer dashboard so that you know that you have to bill a customer for something in the future. It is a non-posting transaction, which means that it has no impact on sales until it is converted to an Invoice.

A Delayed Charge can be created by going to the Customer from **Sales >** (or **Invoicing >)** on the **Left-hand Navigation Bar** and then **[Customers]**. Select your

Customer in the new window and click on Delayed Charge from the **<New transaction ▼ >** dropdown.

> ☝ *Alternatively, click <+ New> and click on **Delayed charge** which can be found under **CUSTOMERS**.*

Enter the details about the transaction that you want to be able to invoice in the future.

Once you have clicked on **<Save and new | ▼ >** and exit out of the screen, it will appear in the customer dashboard with a clickable **ACTION** to **Create invoice ▼** next to it, exactly as we saw with an Estimate.

Click **Create invoice ▼** to see the following Invoice, converted from the Delayed Charge:

You can also add other elements to the same Invoice, such as Estimates that have not yet been invoiced, as seen on the right-hand side. When you click on **Add to Invoice**, you will be presented with the option to bill the remaining amount of the Estimate or just a portion of it. This allows you to combine several charges on one Invoice as can be seen below:

Time Activity

> ➢ *Time Tracking is an advanced feature and beyond the scope of this book. However, in the interests of thoroughly examining the types of transactions, I have included the following.*

This feature allows you to enter the time spent by a consultant, subcontractor, or employee which, similar to a delayed charge, serves as a reminder to invoice the client. A Time Activity can be created by going to the Customer from **Sales >** (or **Invoicing >)** on the **Left-hand Navigation Bar** and then **[Customers]**. Select your Customer in the new window and click on Time Activity from the **<New transaction▼>** dropdown.

The interface is straightforward and requires details that we have discussed in earlier sections:

The one new section is with respect to time. You have two choices:

- ☑ **Enter Start and End Times** to have QBO calculate the time spent.
- Or you may enter the total **Time** in number of hours.
- You can also enter a **Description**. This information will not be transposed on to the Invoice.
- When you are ready to Invoice the client, you would follow the same instructions as for Delayed Charges.

Statement

When a particular Customer has more than one or two unpaid transactions and/or various types of transactions, a Statement allows you to collect all these transactions in one document and send to the Customer.

A Statement for a Customer can be generated by going to **Sales >** (or **Invoicing >**) on the **Left-Hand Navigation Bar**, selecting **[Customers]**, and clicking the Customer name. Click on **<New transaction ▼ >**.

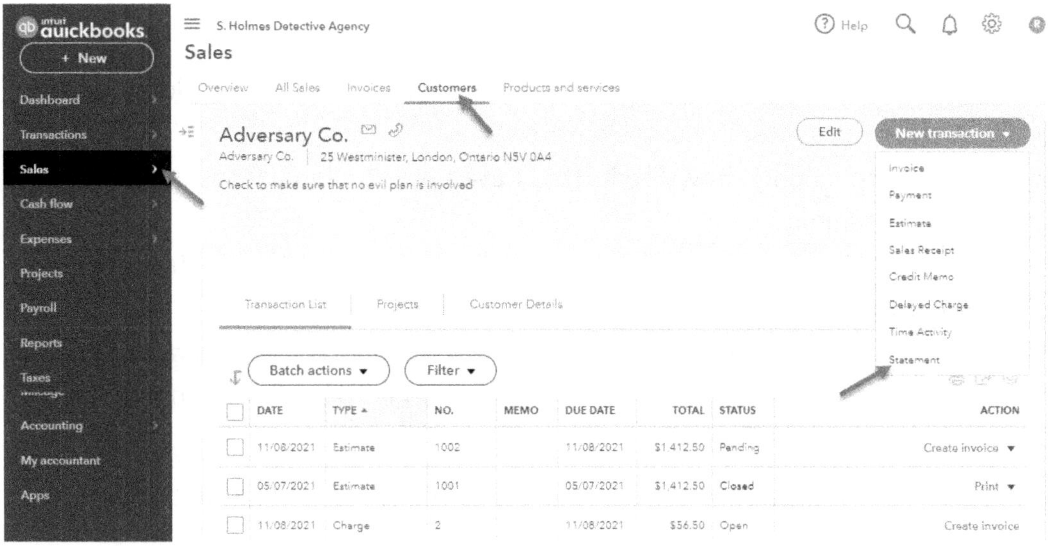

The last option is **Statement**, which, when clicked on, gives you the following screen:

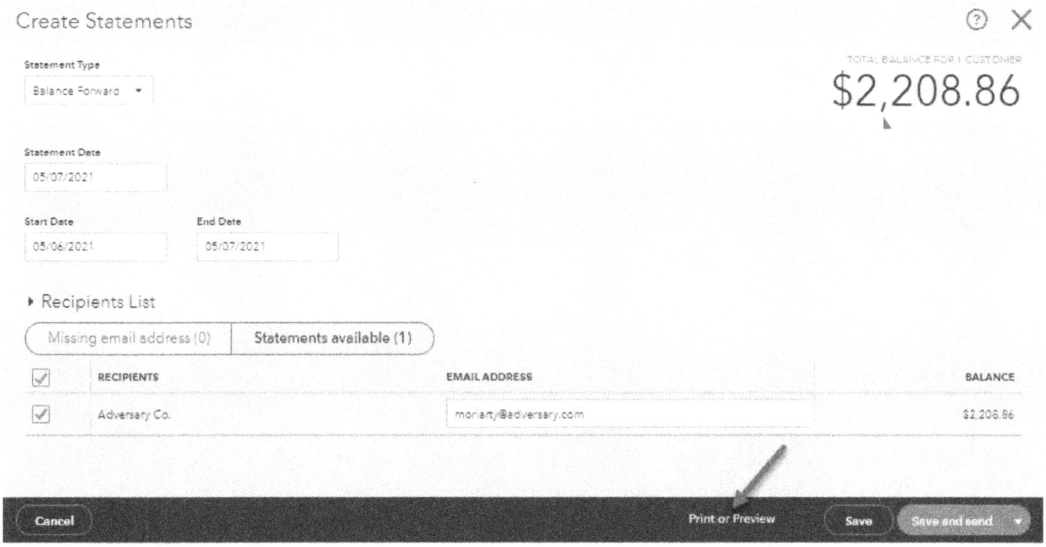

- You can select the **Statement Type▾** that you would like to generate:

- Balance Forward shows the amount owing at a certain date plus transactions after the dates entered.
- Open Items only shows items that have not yet been paid as of the date of the Statement.
- Transaction Statement show each individual transaction for the dates indicated.

- You can choose the **Statement Date** which might be today's date or the end of last month, as well as the **Start Date** and **End Date**, which shows you all transactions for that date range.

Click on **Print or Preview** to see the details that will appear on the statement.

Print Statement

To print, right-click the preview and select Print. Or, click the Print icon if you see one below.

You can then **<Print>** the statement to mail to the customer, or you can exit from this screen and click on **<Save and send ▼ >** to email the statement to the customer.

> ✓ *When you have more than a few Customers with open balances that have not been paid after 30 days, it is good practice to send them regular Statements that remind them of their obligations and improves your chances of getting paid.*

CREATE SUPPLIERS, BILLS, AND EXPENSES

When another entity provides you with a product or service, they are known as a Supplier (or vendor) and the related transaction is referred to as a Bill or an Expense. These are costs that a business incurs to earn revenues and can include direct costs such as the handles for magnifying glasses, salaries paid to Watson or the factory workers, rent for SHDA's office space, and various other expenses. From an accounting perspective, these show up on the Profit and Loss Statement as Cost of Goods Sold if they are direct costs or Expenses if they are indirect costs.

Similar to Customers and Invoices, QBO has a section devoted to Suppliers and Bills/Expenses.

> ➢   *Entering Bills is only available in QBO* Essentials *and* Plus.

The difference between a "Bill" and an "Expense" from an accounting perspective is that a Bill is entered when you receive an Invoice from your supplier, for payment at a later date. Essentially, Bills are recorded on an accrual basis. Expenses, conversely, are entered when you pay for them, and are therefore recorded on a cash basis.

Many businesses, especially service-based businesses, only have a few Expenses during the year and as such it doesn't have a material impact if they only reflect these Expenses in their books on a cash basis, i.e., when they pay for them, as long as the bill date is not too far off from the payment date. Technically, there should be an "accrual" for these Expenses at the end of the fiscal year of the business or another specified accounting period (monthly or quarterly). This means that you add up the Expenses that are incurred prior to the end of the year (or period) but paid for after the year end and set up a Journal Entry to record them as payable.

Setting Up Suppliers

To access the Suppliers, click on **Expenses >** from the **Left-hand Navigation Bar**.
Then click on **[Suppliers]** at the top of the interface.

The first time you set up a supplier you will see the screen below. You have the
option to **<Import suppliers>** or **<Add supplier manually>**.

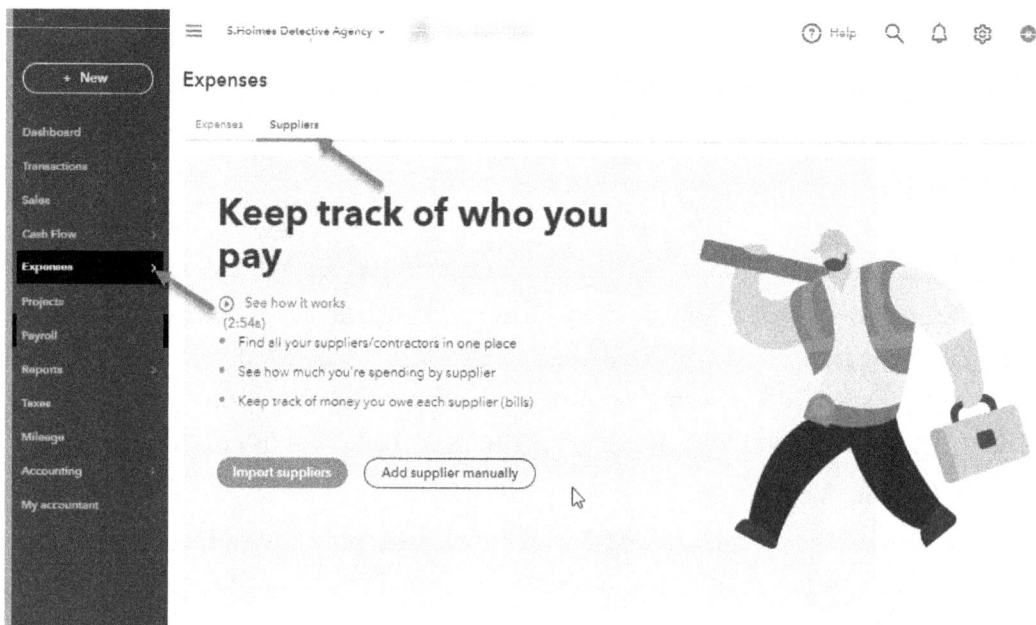

Click on **<Add supplier manually>** after which you will be taken to the supplier
information screen. The screen is similar to the customer setup, although there are
fewer available fields. We'll look at the first half of the screen and then the second.

Supplier Information

Title	First name	Middle name	Last name	Suffix	Email
Ms	Irene		Adler		adler@adlerindustries.ca

Company	Phone	Mobile	Fax
Adler Industries	519-555-1234		

* Display name as

Other | Website

Ms Irene Adler ▼ | | http://adlerindustries.ca

Print on cheque as ☑ Use display name

Billing rate (/hr)

Ms Irene Adler   125.00

Address map   Terms

123 Hudson Ave   Net 30 ▼

Opening balance   as of

London | Ontario | 02/07/2021

Account no.

N5V 0A5 | Canada   Appears in the memo of all payments

Notes   Business ID No. / Social Insurance No.

Send payment via e-transfer. No cheques!

Cancel | Make inactive | Privacy | Save

- **Title**, **First name**, **Middle name**, **Last name**, and **Suffix** allows you to add specific details to identify the Supplier (vendor).
- **Company** is the name of the business, if any.
- **Display name as** allows you to set the name that will be shown in your navigation for this supplier. This is a personal preference and can always be changed. Similar to Customers, you can choose the business name or the name of the business owner or contact.
- **Print on cheque as** specifies the name that will be printed on the cheque. This is sometimes different from the name that you choose for the display name, e.g., if you choose the name of your supplier rather than the name of their business for display purposes, you can use this section to set the actual name that appears on the cheque.
- **Address** of the supplier.
- **Notes** is where you would enter anything that is specific to this supplier that might be pertinent.
- **Email address** of the supplier.

- **Phone**, **Mobile**, and **Fax** numbers. **Other** can hold a phone number, email address, or other point of contact. QBO will automatically format these fields.
- **Website** of the supplier, if applicable. QBO will automatically add "http://" to the website address.
- **Billing rate (/hr)** is used to enter the rate that your vendor might charge on an hourly basis. This is generally applicable to subcontractors and other service businesses that bill you by the hour.
- **Terms ▾** represent the amount of time within which the Bill has to be paid. Some Suppliers will give you a discount for paying early.
- **Opening balance** is applicable if you are transitioning from another accounting software and you have an amount payable to the supplier. You can also enter the **as of** date on which the balance was payable. If an amount is entered here, QBO will automatically create an entry to an account that is automatically created in the Equity section of your chart of accounts called Opening Balance Equity. It will also show up on your Accounts Payable report, which shows the amounts owing to Suppliers. My recommendation is to enter supplier balances via a Journal Entry rather than entering the balances here to avoid issues with your accounting.
- **Account no.** can be assigned by you to help manage Suppliers when you have more than a few. This appears on the memo section of payments including cheques.
- **Business ID No. / Social Insurance No.** of the supplier can be entered, which is mainly used to create tax slips at the end of the year. QBO allows you to create T4As for subcontractors and T5018s for subcontractors who specifically work in construction. The actual creation of the tax slips is an advanced topic and beyond the scope of this book.

Supplier Information

NSV 0A5	Canada

Notes

Send payment via e-transfer. No cheques!

📎 Attachments   Maximum size: 20MB

Drag/Drop files here or click the icon

Appears in the memo of all payments

Business ID No. / Social Insurance No.

Supplier Type ⓘ

Business ▾

Track for T4A / T5018

Do not track ▾

Default expense account

Legal and professional f ▾

Get custom fields with Advanced

Custom fields let you add more detailed info about your
customers and transactions.
Sort, track, and report info that's important to you.

Learn more

(Cancel) (Make inactive)   Privacy   (**Save**)

- **Supplier Type ▾** lets you choose Business or Individual. This relates to the business ID field; if you have entered a business ID number, then you would select Business. If you enter a SIN, then you would select Individual. This field is also used for tax reporting.

- **Track for T4A/T5018 ▾** has three options - Do not track, T4A and T5018 where you can create tax slips directly from QBO when selected. If you do plan to create these tax slips, then you must enter the business ID or SIN.

- **Default expense account ▾** allows you enter an Expense categorization that will then appear automatically on all Bills or Expenses created for this Supplier. This is a useful time saver when the same categorization is used for all transactions relating to this Supplier. For example, Irene Adler provides consulting services, which can be categorized under Legal and professional fees.

Once you have entered all the necessary information, click **<Save>** to enter the record.

> ✓   *Not all fields have to be entered, and they can always be edited later, <u>except</u>*
>   *<u>for the opening balance field</u>, which cannot be edited. In fact, only the name*
>   *of the Supplier needs to be entered, which is useful for Suppliers who simply*
>   *issue receipts, such as retail stores.*

After you have clicked on **<Save>**, you will be brought to your **Suppliers** screen
where you can see a list of all the Suppliers that you have entered.

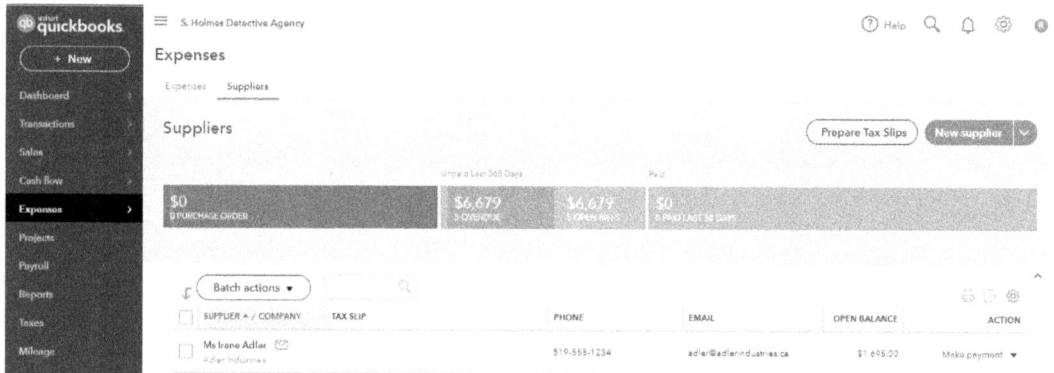

Create a Bill for a Supplier (Essentials and Plus)

A Bill is an Invoice given to you by a supplier that must be paid by a certain date.
You would enter the Bill in QBO when received. QBO then records it as an Expense
based on the account categorization that you select. It will also be recorded as an
Accounts Payable, which is an amount that is payable to the Supplier. When you
pay the Bill, QBO reflects the transaction as having been paid from the relevant
bank or credit card account and the corresponding Accounts Payable is eliminated
(or reduced in the case of partial payment).

To create a Bill, click **Expenses >** on the **Left-hand Navigation Bar** and click on
[Expenses]. From here, click on **<New transaction ▼ >** and select Bill from the
dropdown:

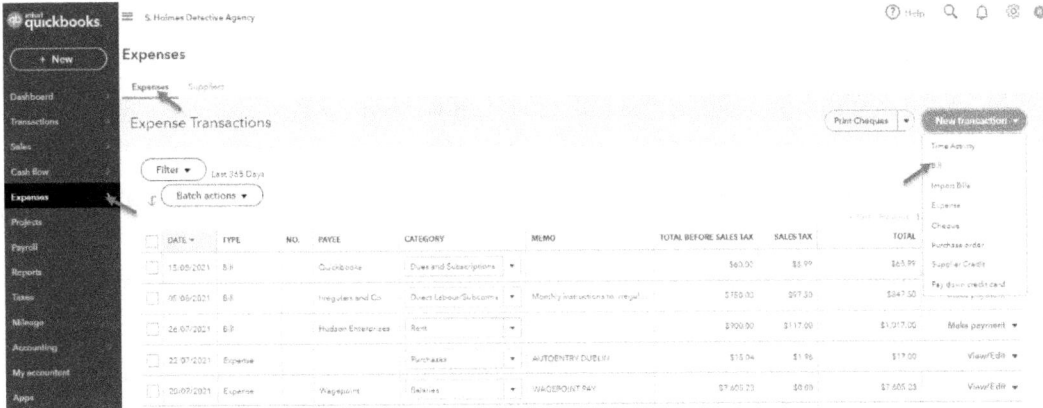

> ⚡ *You can also click on* **<+ New>** *button on the top left-hand corner and select* **Bill** *from the* **SUPPLIERS** *column.*

A completed Bill looks like the below:

- **Supplier** is the name of the Supplier that we created above for Irene Adler.
- **Mailing address** prepopulates with the information entered when we created the supplier. You can change this information directly in the Bill. If you do change the information directly on the Bill, note that it will not update the Supplier record.

- **Terms▼** also prepopulates with the information from when you set up the supplier. This can also be changed here.
- **Bill date** is indicated on the Bill itself and should be entered. You can use the calendar provided by QBO to select the date or type it in manually using the date format that was set up in the Other preferences section of the Advanced tab in Account and settings.
- **Due date** is calculated automatically when the terms are entered by adding the number of days indicated in the terms to the bill date.
- **Bill no.** will be a number on the Bill that you receive from your supplier. Although this field is optional, entering it helps you identify the bill in the future especially when you have more than a few bills from the same supplier.
- **Location▼** is additional type of categorization offered by QBO. This is an advanced topic and beyond the scope of this book.
- **Tags** can be used to report on transactions with similar characteristics. You can add more than one tag.
- **Amounts are▼** gives you a dropdown as follows:

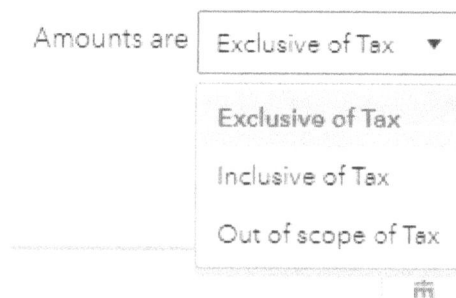

Amounts are | Exclusive of Tax ▼

Exclusive of Tax

Inclusive of Tax

Out of scope of Tax

  ○ Amounts are Exclusive of Tax when you enter the net amount of the Bill and add the tax on top of it.
  ○ Inclusive of Tax means that the full amount of the Bill is entered.
  ○ Out of scope of Tax means that sales tax does not apply at all.
- **CATEGORY** represents the account from the Chart of Accounts to which this Bill relates. Each Bill needs to be allocated to a specific account. In this case, since we indicated the Expense category for Ms. Adler when we set her up as a Supplier, this is automatically assigned. We can change it in the event that this particular bill should be applied to a different account.

> ➢ *A typical Bill will always be allocated to Accounts Payable in an accounting software, which means that the Bill is payable at a later date. Since every transaction must have a debit and a credit, the debit side of a Bill must be the account category which is usually an Expense but can also be another category such as asset or liability, depending on the nature of the transaction.*

- **DESCRIPTION** is optional and is based on the details on the Bill. This can give you insight into what this Bill related to in the future when you need to jog your memory.
- **AMOUNT** is the total or the net amount that is indicated on the Bill, depending on whether you choose Exclusive of Tax or Inclusive of Tax. If you choose Out of scope of Tax then the net amount and total amount will be the same.
- **SALES TAX▼** is a code that is selected from the dropdown. QBO then calculates the amount of the sales tax applicable based on the code selected, automatically.

AMOUNT	SALES TAX
68.99	HST ON ▼
	HST PE 2016 (15%)
	Zero-rated (0%)
	Exempt (0%)
	Out of Scope (0%)
	HST ON (13%)
	HST NS (15%)
	GST (5%)
	GST/QST QC - 9.975 (14.975%)
	QST QC - 9.975 (9.975%)

> ➤ *To enter a Bill that has both taxable and non-taxable amounts, you would enter the taxable amount on one line and the non-taxable amount on the line below along with the relevant tax code.*

- ☑ **BILLABLE** when ticked indicates whether it is going to be billed to a Customer. If you check this box here, you will be able to add the Bill directly on the Invoice to the Customer without having to re-enter it.
- **CUSTOMER** allows you to enter a Customer to which the Bill relates. There will then appear an option to add the details of the Bill to an Invoice to the Customer.
- **<Save>** allows you to save the Bill once all the information is entered.
- **More** becomes available on the **Bottom Bar** after you click on **<Save>**. The following options are available:
- Copy the Bill will make a duplicate is useful if you have a similar Bill to enter. Once a copy is created, you can go ahead and edit the details and save it as a new Bill.
- Delete allows you to delete the Bill.
- Transaction journal shows you the allocation of Debits and Credits and is useful to see what accounts the Bill is being allocated to.
- Audit history allows you to see when the Bill was entered and any subsequent modifications, by user.
- **<Save and new | ▼ >** takes you to a new transaction if you are entering more than one Bill. Clicking the down arrow will give you the following dropdown options:
- Save and close takes you out of the Bill window.

Enter Payments

Once you have entered a Bill, it will remain as an Accounts Payable until it is actually paid.

Similar to paying an Invoice, there are several ways to "pay" a Bill:

1. Enter a payment manually.
2. Match from your banking downloads.
3. Find a match.
4. Use the **Pay bills** interface.

Enter Payment Manually

Click on Expenses > Expenses in the Left-hand Navigation Bar.

A payment can be recorded by clicking on **Make payment ▼** next to the Bill itself under **ACTION**.

When you click on **Make payment ▼** next to the Bill, the screen below will pop up, which is usually fully prepopulated by QBO:

- **Payee** is the name of the Supplier associated with the Bill you are paying.
- **Email** is their email address.

- **Bank/Credit account** should be carefully verified to ensure that the correct account from which payment is to be made is being selected.
- **Mailing address** is the address of the Supplier, which prepopulates if it is included in the Supplier details.
- **Payment date** usually reflect today's date. This can be changed to the past or future.
- **Ref no.** is the cheque number or any other reference number. This can also be left blank if payment is by debit or credit card.
- **Print later** indicates that you can print the payment later as part of a batch. This is useful when you are issuing several cheques on one date.

The body of the payment screen will show all outstanding Bills for this Supplier. Each can then be checked or unchecked depending on which Bills are being paid.

- **DESCRIPTION** shows the bill number from the actual Bill.
- **DUE DATE** is the due date from the actual Bill.
- **ORIGINAL AMOUNT** is the amount from the actual Bill.
- **OPEN BALANCE** is the amount that has not yet been paid. If you have already made a partial payment, this amount will be less than the original amount.
- **PAYMENT** is where you enter the amount being paid which can be the full amount, an amount less than the open balance or an amount greater than the open balance (which will then be recorded as a credit).
- **Amount** shows the amount of the Bill(s) being paid.
- **Amount to Apply** to is the amount being applied to the Bill.
- **Amount to Credit** are any overpayments.
- **Memo** can be any notes that you might want to make on this specific payment.
- **Attachments** can include copies of the Bill, special instructions, etc.
- **Print or preview** in the **Bottom Bar** allows you either Print Remittance Slip that you can send to the supplier or Print cheque using preprinted cheques
- **<Save and new| ▼ >** takes you to a new payment. The down arrow opens a dropdown with the following options:
- Save and close exits you from the transaction.

> ✓   *When you click <Save and new| ▼> a new blank transaction will appear.*
> *You would then enter **Payee** ▼ from the dropdown on the top left to bring up*
> *all the Bills owing to that particular Supplier.*

Match from Banking Download

If you have set up your banking transactions to download automatically, and the
amount of the payment deposited into your bank account EXACTLY matches the
amount of the Bill, you will usually see a green highlighted **1 record found**
notification over the item and the option to match it. To access the banking
interface, go to the **Left-hand Navigation Bar**, click **Transactions >** and **[Banking]**. If
you have a payment that matches the amount of the bill, you will see the following:

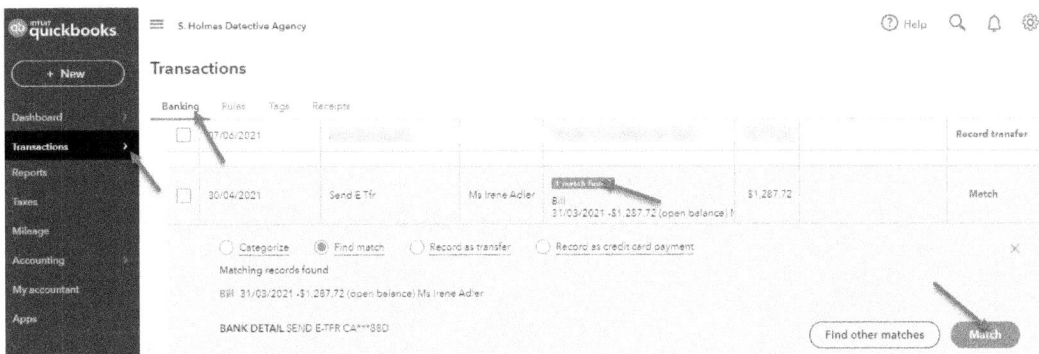

Review the details in the banking transaction to make sure that the payment is in
fact for the Bill to which it is matched. Once confirmed, click on **<Match>** and the
payment is then automatically entered.

Find a Match

The process for matching payments to existing Bills is the same as for Invoices and
discussed in this section.

Pay bills

QBO has an interface whereby you can record payment and initiate the cheque
printing process for several bills at the same time. This is a useful time saving
mechanism when you have more than a couple of bills.

To access this feature, click on **<+ New>** button on the top left-hand corner and
select **Pay bills** from the **SUPPLIERS** column.

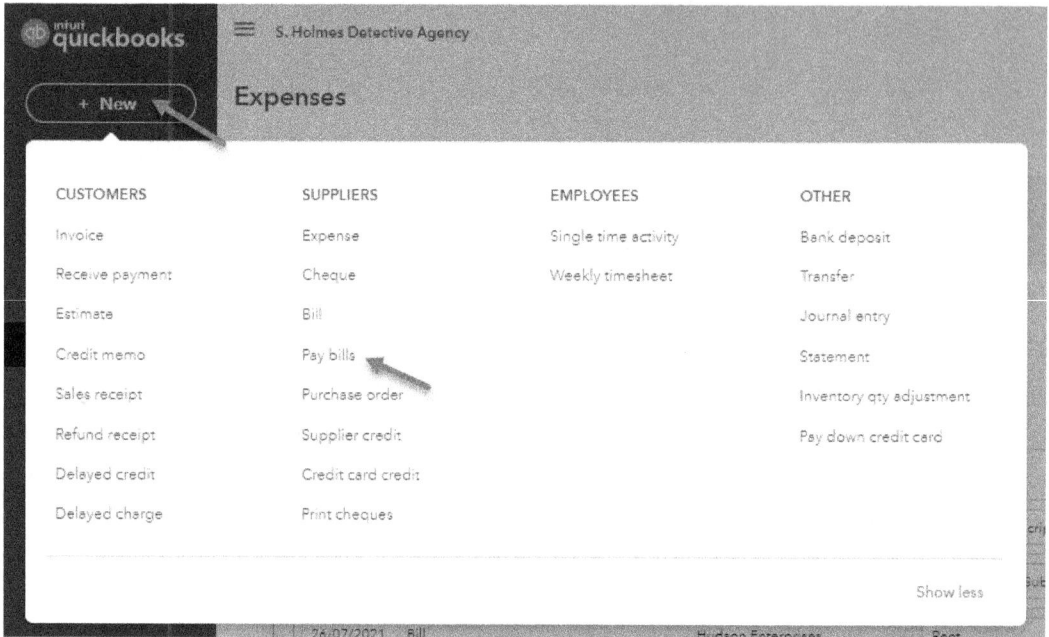

- **Payment account** is the account from which the bill will be paid from.
- **Balance** shows you the balance in the bank account selected in Payment account.
- **Payment date** is the date on which the bill will be paid (this can be future dated).

- **Starting cheque no.** corresponds to your pre-printed cheques. If you are simply recording bill payments, you do not have to enter anything here.
- **Print later** simply adds it to a queue of cheques which is discussed in the section on Print Cheques.
- **TOTAL PAYMENT AMOUNT** is the total of bills that you are paying
- ☑ lets you select the bills which you want to pay by clicking on the check box.
- **PAYEE/REF NO>/DUE DATE** are from directly from the Bill.
- **OPEN BALANCE** shows the amount of the bill that has not yet been paid.
- **CREDIT APPLIED** shows you if there are any credits available for the Supplier. If so, an amount can be entered here.
- **PAYMENT** is the amount of the bill being paid. This can be any amount up to the full amount of the bill.
- **TOTAL AMOUNT** is the same as the PAYMENT amount.
- **Current account** balance is the balance in the bank account from which you are paying the bill.
- **Total payment** is deducted from the current account balance.
- **New account balance** shows you the balance after the total payment has been deducted.
- **<Save and print| ▼ >** when clicked will take you the Print cheques screen where you would follow the instructions as per the section on Print cheques.
- Save simply records the transactions(s), but you remain on the same screen.
- Save and close records the transaction(s) and exits you from the screen.

Other Types of Expense Transactions

There are several other types of transactions that are available in this section. Let's review each one of these which you can access by going to the **Left-hand Navigation Bar**, clicking on **Expenses >** and then **<New transaction ▼ >** in the window that opens. Choose the type of transaction from the dropdown.

Time Activity

This is an advanced topic and beyond the scope of this book.

Expense

There are a variety of Expenses for which you do not need to necessarily enter both a Bill and a payment. Rather an Expense, similar to a Sales Receipt, combines the Bill and payment into one transaction. This is appropriate for transactions that you incur and pay at the same time, e.g., purchases from a retail store or monthly subscriptions. Some businesses may only have a handful of Expenses in which case entering Bills may not be necessary, especially if you don't have to keep track of how much you owe to Suppliers.

To create an Expense, click **Expenses >** on the **Left-hand Navigation Bar** and click on **[Expenses]**. From here, click on **<New transaction▼ >** and select Expense from the dropdown:

> ↻ *You can also click on <+ New> button on the top left-hand corner and select* **Expense** *from the* **SUPPLIERS** *column.*

The **Expense** window opens:

Most of the fields here are similar to a Bill, except for the following differences:

- Terms are not reflected here since an Expense transaction innately assumes that you are paying the amount at the time it is entered.
- Bill date is replaced by Payment date.
- **Due date** is irrelevant since the Expense is paid right away.
- **Bill no**. is replaced by **Ref no.** which can be a bill number or any other reference that makes sense. You can also leave this blank.

All other fields remain the same as a Bill.

The other way to enter Expenses, and the easiest, is to enter them directly through
the banking transaction download discussed in our section on entering banking
transactions. Since the transactions download automatically, entering them directly
through the **Left-hand Navigation Bar → Transactions > →** Banking dashboard
saves a great deal of time on data entry rather than entering them manually.
Ideally, manual entry of Expenses is limited to when you are entering Expenses for
accounts that are not connected through online banking, such as the occasional
Expenses that you incur through your personal bank or credit card account.

Cheque

To create a transaction which you would like to pay by cheque, click **Expenses >** on
the **Left-hand Navigation Bar** and click on **[Expenses]**. From here, click on **<New
transaction ▾ >** and select Cheque from the dropdown:

Cheque transactions are identical to Expenses except that they have a field for
Cheque no. on them. These are used when you want to pay by, and print cheques.

From here, follow the instructions found under the section on creating an Expense.

Print Cheques

QBO allows you to create and print cheques directly onto pre-formatted cheques.
This can be done after you have created a bill payment.

The bottom of the screen has an option to click on Print or Preview directly from the payment:

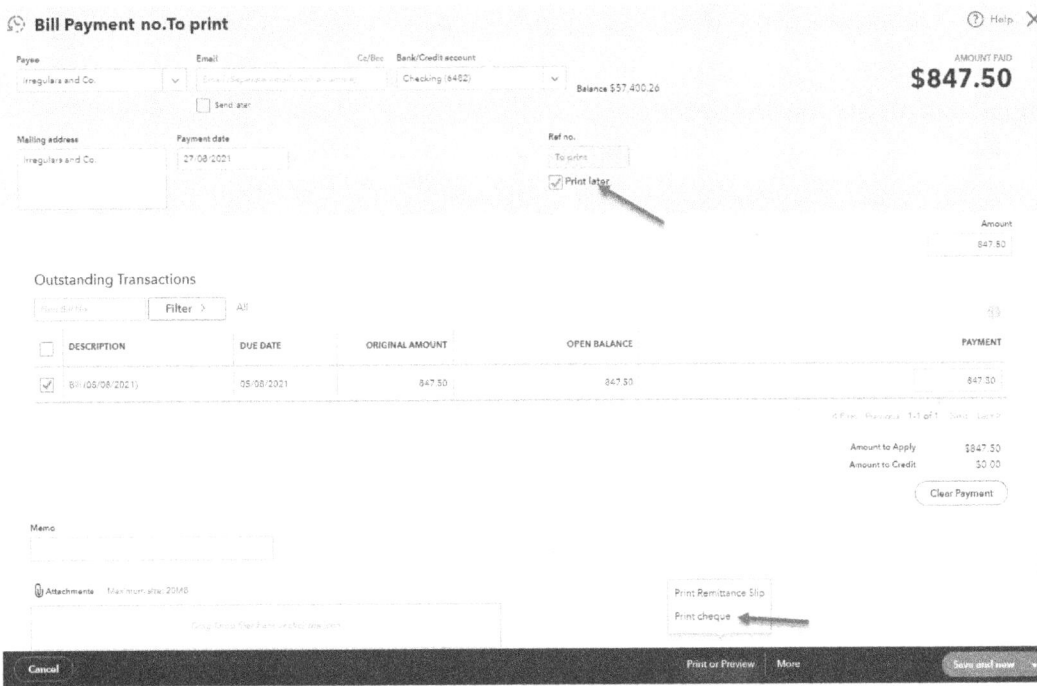

You can check the box next to **Print Later** to set the cheque up in a queue for printing.

To initiate the Print cheque process, click on Print cheque found in dropdown for **Print or Preview** at the bottom of the screen. You will see the following:

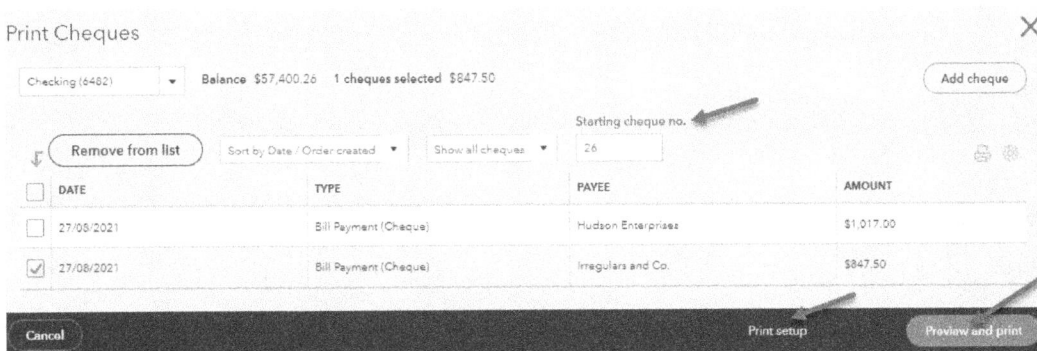

This interface shows you the list of all cheques that are ready to be printed. You can add as many as you like to a batch either through pay bills or creating a **Cheque** transaction as explained earlier in this section.

- ☑ You can check the box next to the cheques that you like to print.
- Enter the Starting cheque no.

Click on **<Preview and Print>** to see what your cheque will look like and then go ahead and print it from the print preview screen. (Make sure that the preprinted cheque forms are in the printer!)

> ➢ *If you have issues with the appearance of the cheque, you can go to Print setup to verify your settings.*

Purchase Order (Plus)

A Purchase Order (PO) is typically used by businesses that sell products. A Purchase Order reflects details about items being purchased and is sent by the business to a Supplier who then fulfills the Purchase Order in whole or in part. This is a non posting transaction in QBO, which means that QBO does not record it as a transaction; rather it is for informational purposes only. Once a Purchase Order has been fulfilled by the supplier, it can be converted into a Bill, in whole or in part, without having to re-enter the details.

To create a PO, click **Expenses >** on the **Left-hand Navigation Bar** and click on **[Expenses]**. From here, click on **<New transaction▼ >** and select Purchase Order from the dropdown:

> ⚟ *You can also click on* **<+ New>** *button on the top left-hand corner and select* **Purchase order** *from the SUPPLIERS column.*

The **Purchase Order** screen will open:

The main difference with a PO is that the date field is now referred to as **Purchase Order date**.

Once you have entered the details pertaining to the purchase order, click on **<Save>**. You will see that a new **<Copy to Bill>** button appears:

The **<Copy to Bill>** button allows you to create a bill directly from the PO.

Supplier Credit

There are various reasons you might receive a credit from a Supplier:

- Products purchased are defective or incomplete.
- Services received were incomplete or not as indicated.
- You return an item that you decide you no longer require.
- A product is no longer in stock.
- A refund or a discount is given after the product or service is purchased.

A Supplier Credit is recorded after the full amount of the Bill or Expense has been entered. It is a separate transaction that either reduces the amount payable to the supplier now or in the future or in anticipation of a refund.

To create Supplier Credit, click **Expenses >** on the **Left-hand Navigation Bar** and click on **[Expenses]**. From here, click on **<New transaction ▼ >** and select Supplier Credit from the dropdown:

> ⇅ *You can also click on* **<+ New>** *button on the top left-hand corner and select* ***Supplier credit*** *from the* ***SUPPLIERS*** *column.*

The **Supplier Credit** window will open:

The details on the supplier credit are very similar to a Bill or Expense. Once entered, they will show up as a negative amount in the **Expenses** dashboard. They can then be used to offset payments to a Supplier as discussed in the Enter Payments section.

Pay down credit card

QBO has a separate transaction type for payment of a credit card. This is simply a transfer from your business bank account to your business credit card account.

ENTER BANKING TRANSACTIONS AND CREATE RULES

One of the most powerful features of QBO for the small business user is the reduction in data entry that comes along with the ability to download your transactions from your business bank and credit card accounts. Once you have linked your business accounts per instructions in the section on connecting your bank accounts, transactions will automatically download into a staging area on a daily basis. Each downloaded transaction includes most of the information relating to the transaction that is available to the bank.

> ✓   *It is important to check that transactions are downloading regularly (minimally on a monthly basis). Sometimes QBO inexplicably stops downloading the transactions automatically. In this case you simply need to click on **<Update>** to re-trigger the download. If you change your password or login details, then the transactions will stop downloading until you update these details in QBO.*

To access the banking screen, click on **Transactions >** (appearing as **Banking >** in some versions of QBO) from the **Left-hand Navigation Bar**. This will take you to the following screen:

1. These are the different tabs that are available on this page. We will discuss **[Rules]**, **[Tags]**, and **[Receipts]** below.
2. **<Link account | ▼ >** is where you click to add a new account, discussed in detail in the banking set up section.
3. **<⟳Update>** allows you to re-trigger a download when it has stopped updating. Ideally, QBO downloads transactions on a daily basis but sometimes it stops downloading. You can also use this function to bring in the most recent transactions.
4. This section shows all the accounts that have been linked. It also shows you the balance according to your bank and the balance in QuickBooks. The difference should only ever be the transactions that have not yet been entered. Once all transactions that have been downloaded are entered, then these two balances should be identical. If not, there could be various reasons for this which are discussed in greater detail in Reconcile Bank and Credit Card Accounts section. There is also a number in orange that indicates the number of uncategorized transactions.
5. There are three tabs here: **[For review]** will show transactions that have not yet been categorized. **[Categorized]** shows you all transactions that have been categorized, i.e., entered into QuickBooks. **[Excluded]** are transactions that you have discarded, which should be used carefully.
6. This section allows you to filter by **Dates ▼**, **Transactions ▼**, or simply **🔍 Search** for a transaction.
7. This is the section where individual transactions are downloaded. There are descriptors for each transaction and include:

- **DATE** which is automatically downloaded.
- **DESCRIPTION** is provided by the bank but can be added to or changed.
- **PAYEE** is the Supplier, Customer or other entity that you have transacted with.
- **CATEGORY OR MATCH** is the account category in which the transaction is classified in QBO. These account categories are set up and can be found in the Chart of Accounts. QBO will often automatically assign a category based on its best guess. This is frequently incorrect and should be reviewed to ensure that the category is accurate.
- **TAX** are the sales tax codes that apply to a transaction. These are available via a dropdown.

- **SPENT** are amounts that are withdrawn from the bank/credit card account and are automatically downloaded.
- **RECEIVED** are amounts that are received into the bank account and are also automatically downloaded.
- **ACTION** allows you to:
- **Add** a transaction that has not already been entered into QBO.
- **Match** a transaction that has already been entered and QBO is simply confirming that it agrees to this transaction. Additionally, QBO will automatically match a payment to an Invoice or to a Bill if the amounts are identical. This is very useful as it means that you do not have to enter a separate transaction.
- **Record transfer** is generally a transfer between Balance Sheet accounts.
- The ☑**Checkbox**, per the image below, allows you to select all transactions on the page. Alternatively, you can check individual transactions by clicking on the ☑**Checkbox** next to it. When you do click on the ☑**Checkbox**, you will see the following:

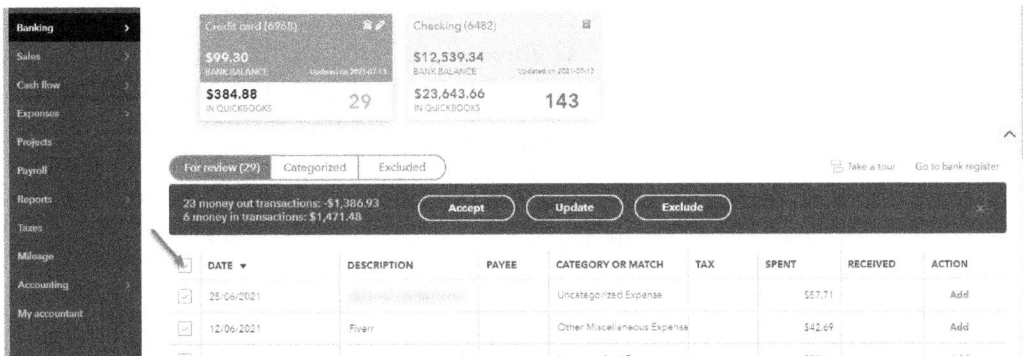

Your choices are to:

- **<Accept>** one or multiple payments based on the information in the transaction. When you **<Accept>** the transaction, QBO will record it.
- **<Update>** one or multiple payments by entering the information relating to the transaction(s). This is useful when you have several transactions that have the same payee, account and tax category. Clicking on **<Update>**shows you the screen below:

Update Selected

Payee   Category

Adversary Co.   ▼   Select category   ▼

Class   Location   TAX

Select class   ▼   Select location   ▼   HST ON

Tax   HST ON

Select tax   ⌄

Cancel   (Apply)   (Apply and accept)   HST ON

                                                                         HST ON

You can choose to update just one or more of the fields that apply to the selected transactions. Once you have filled out the fields, you can choose **<Apply>** which will make the change but will not add the transaction (it will remain in the Banking interface) or **<Apply and accept>** which will add the transaction and reflect it as Categorized.

- **<Exclude>** transactions, which, as mentioned, should only be used on a limited basis to eliminate duplicates or a transaction that has already been entered manually.

How to Enter Banking Transactions

When entering transactions through the banking download it is important that transactions are not duplicated. This means that transactions that have already been entered should be matched rather than added. This applies to transactions such as:

- Bills and bill payments.
- Invoices and invoice payments.
- Expenses that are set up manually rather than through the banking download.
- Transfers between accounts.

Creating an Expense

To enter a transaction, click anywhere on the transaction (except on **Add** or any other **ACTION**). This will expand the transaction:

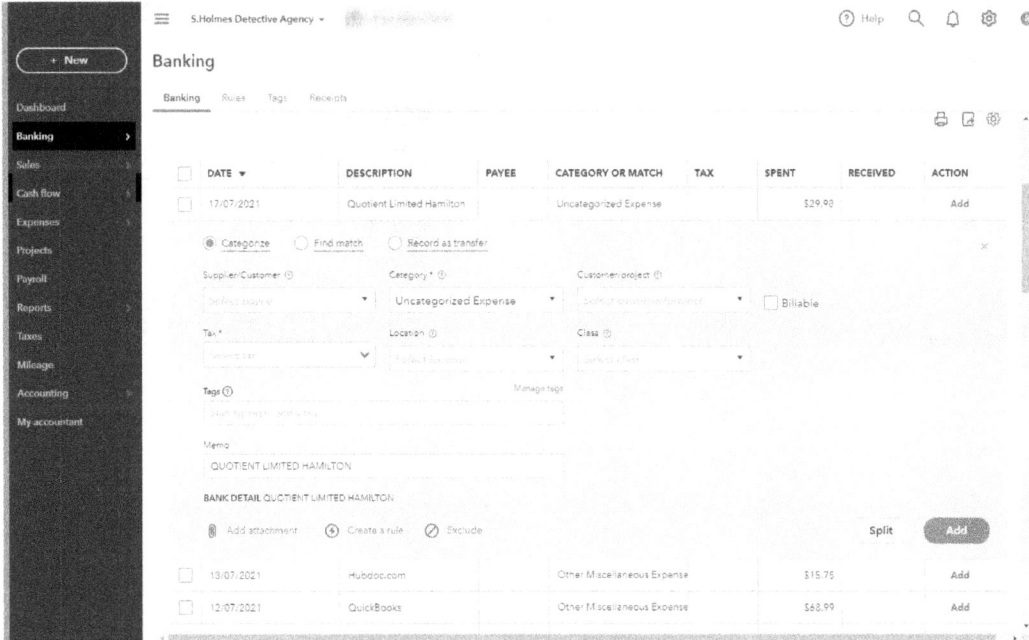

You will see that the **DATE**, **Category**, and **Memo** have been automatically populated with information provided by the bank.

❖ **Example:**

This transaction is for a proposal software that Mr. Watson uses to send quotes to potential clients and is paid on a monthly basis.

◆ *The name of the supplier is Quotient, which he adds directly here rather than going to Suppliers and creating a new supplier.*

◆ *To do this he types "Quotient" into the **Supplier/Customer** field and waits for a couple of seconds for QBO to ask him if he wants to add them as a Supplier.*

◆ *He clicks on **<Save>** after which Quotient is permanently added as a Supplier. In the future, he only has to type in the first couple of letters and "Quotient" will be available as a dropdown.*

◆ *The account category that Mr. Watson likes to use for these types of subscriptions is the "dues and subscriptions" account. He types it in and realizes that it is not available as a dropdown in the account. Consequently, he decides to add it as account directly from here rather than going to Chart of Accounts. He types in "dues and subscriptions". QBO opens up the Chart of Accounts screen and asks him for the details relating to the account. Since dues and subscriptions is an Expense, he chooses this. It is also specifically available as the detail type. He doesn't enter account numbers as he is not using these at this stage, but he might decide to change it later. He also does not enter a default tax code here.*

◆ *Since this is a General Expense, he doesn't enter anything in the customer, location, class, nor tag (he leaves them blank).*

❖   ***Example, continued:***

*He does have to enter **Tax ▼** from the dropdown available. Since this service is based in the US, they don't charge him tax. In this case he uses the* Exempt *tax code. QBO asks him if he wants this to be the default tax code for the dues and subscription category to which he decides, since most of the services he uses do not charge sales tax, to accept the default suggestion. He figures he can always change this for Suppliers that do charge tax.*

◆   *He adds "July" to the prepopulated **Memo** so that it now says, "Quotient Limited Hamilton July".*

◆   *He does a quick review and since everything looks good, he clicks **<Add>**. It is now added into QBO.*

◆   *To verify the transaction that he just added he goes to **[Categorized]** transactions and to his satisfaction he sees that it is there. He clicks on it and notes that he can **Undo** the transaction if he so chooses to in the future. Undoing the transaction will simply move it back into the **[For review]** section where he can enter it again.*

Transactions

Banking   Rules   Tags   Receipts

▣ Amex Gold ⌄   (Link account)(⌄)(⟳ Update)

Amex Gold		Credit card (6968)		Checking (6482)	
$737.28 BANK BALANCE	Updated 19 hours ago	$150.59 BANK BALANCE	Updated 8 hours ago	$28,231.43 BANK BALANCE	Updated 8 hours ago
$6,742.67 IN QUICKBOOKS	126	$111.87 IN QUICKBOOKS	37	$60,989.39 IN QUICKBOOKS	59

(For review (126))(**Categorized**)(Excluded)   ⛶ Take a tour   Go to bank register

(📅 All dates ⌄)(⇅ All transactions ⌄)(🔍 Search by description or check number)

🖶 🗋 ⚙

☐	DATE ▼	DESCRIPTION	AMOUNT	ADDED OR MATCHED	RULE	ACTION
☐	22/07/2021	Autoentry Dublin	-$17.00	Added to: Expense: Purchases 22/07/2021 $17.0		Undo
☐	20/07/2021	Amazon	-$11.49	Added to: Credit Card Expense: Office Expenses		Undo
☐	17/07/2021	Quotient Limited Hamilton	-$29.98	Added to: Expense: Dues and Subscriptions 17/0		Undo

Once you have entered a transaction, QBO will remember the different fields as long as the description of the transaction (in the memo field) is the same.

It will also prompt you to set up rules for transactions. This is useful for recurring transactions or transactions that are always allocated to the same account. As long as there is a common identifying descriptor that is specific to this type of transaction, setting up rules can be a huge time saver. In this case, you would set up a rule for all transactions that have "Quotient" in the **Memo** field. See section on Rules.

Direct Matching to a Transaction Already Entered

QBO recognizes transactions that have already been entered and will automatically match downloaded transactions to them.

The transaction above was entered as a Bill. QBO sees that the amount of $68.99 matches to a Bill that was already entered and gives you the option to match the payment from the banking download to the Bill rather than entering the payment separately. You can expand the transaction to verify that the **1 match found** correctly identifies the Bill that is being paid. If so, you can go ahead and click **<Match>** and QBO automatically records the payment.

Note that the payment amount must be identical to the bill amount. If there is even a $0.01 difference, it will not automatically match. There is however a way to resolve this that involves a couple of additional steps.

Matching to Multiple Transactions

Sometimes a payment is made towards more than one Bill, or a deposit is received for two or more Invoices. In this case, QBO allows you to match the payment or deposit using the steps below:

Expand the transaction by clicking on it anywhere (except on an **ACTION**).

Click on ⦿ **Find match**.

A new window opens up that shows all outstanding Invoices—those that haven't been paid. Since this relates to a "received" amount which represents a deposit (money coming in) QBO will only show outstanding invoices (invoices that have not been paid) here.

Simply click the ☑**Checkbox** next to the Invoices or Bills that were paid. The **Total** should correspond to the amount deposited, leaving a **Difference** of $0.00. Enter the transaction by clicking on **<Save>**.

	DATE	TYPE		REF NUMBER		PAYEE	TRANSACTION AMOUNT	OPEN BALANCE	PAYMENT
☐	30/06/2021	Invoice deposit				Adversary Co	$500.00		
☐	21/06/2021	Invoice		304080		Adversary Co	$219.63	$116.64	
☐	30/06/2021	Invoice		304082		Adversary Co	$679.72	$679.72	
☐	05/07/2021	Invoice		304084		Adversary Co	$141.25	$141.25	
☑	05/07/2021	Invoice		304085		Adversary Co	$1,327.75	$1,327.75	1,327.75
☑	18/07/2021	Invoice		304086		Hooper Inc	$396.89	$396.89	396.88

2 Selected transaction(s) Show | Remove $1,724.63
Downloaded transaction $1,724.63
Resolve ⬤ | Difference $0.00
Total $1,724.63

Mobile Deposit
MOBILE DEPOSIT
12/07/2021 $1,724.63

Match transactions

Show: All   Search   From: 13/04/2021   To: 22/07/2021
Select transaction to match

Cancel   Save

⚠ *If you have received or made a payment against an existing Bill or Invoice, and it doesn't show **Match** in the existing download, you might be tempted to **Add** it as a deposit or Expense. Resist the urge! This is incorrect and will end up double counting the sale or the Expense. This is because when the Bill or Invoice is entered, it is categorized as a sale or Expense. The other side of this transaction is Accounts Payable or Accounts Receivable. When the payment is made, it has to be allocated to Accounts Payable or Receivable (to reduce it) and decrease or increase the balance in your bank account. If you **Add** it, QBO will allocate it to Expense rather than reducing the Accounts Payable or Receivable, which results in duplication.*

Rules

Rules are another great time saving feature that allow you to automate entry of banking transactions. By creating a specific set of criteria, QBO will automatically recognize and populate the downloaded bank transaction. You then have the option to either have QBO enter it automatically or leave it for you to review and add.

When to Use Rules

- Bank charges including amounts charged by your bank for monthly or per transaction fees.
- Interest expense on loans or credit cards.
- Recurring monthly subscriptions for software, apps, magazines etc.

How to Set Up a Rule

From the **Left-hand Navigation Bar**, click **Transactions >** (or **Banking >**). In the window that opens, click **[Rules]**.

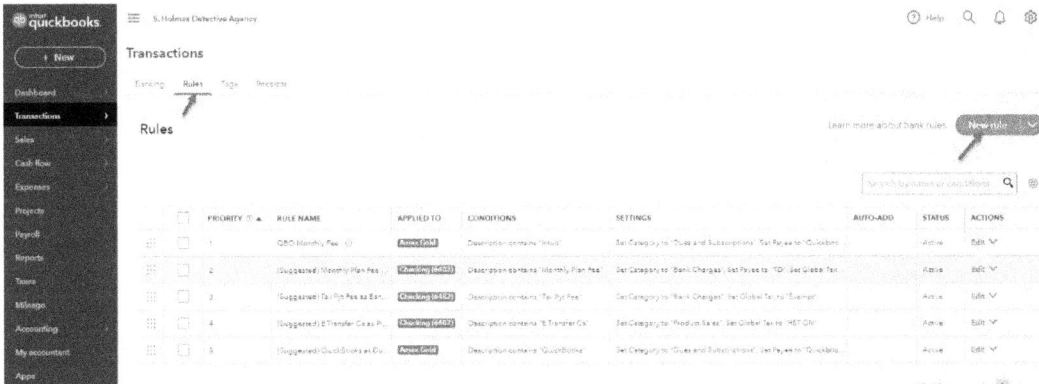

Click on **<New rule| ▼ >** in the top right corner.

The **Create rule** window will open.

What do you want to call this rule? *

QBO Monthly Fee

Apply this to transactions that are

Money out   in   Amex Gold

and include the following: All

Description   Contains   Intuit

+ Add a condition

SETTINGS

should happen when condition

Then Assign

Transaction type   Expense

Category   Dues and Subscriptions   Add a split

Payee   Quickbooks

Tax   HST ON (13%)

Tags   Start typing to add a tag

+ Assign more

Automatically confirm transactions this rule applies to

Auto-add

Cancel   Save

- **What do you want to call this rule?** Create a name for the Rule in the box so that it is easily recognizable.

- Choose to Apply this to transactions that are ▼ either:
- Money out for payments that are spent out of the bank or credit card account, or
- Money in, which includes deposits and payments received into the bank or credit card account.
- Use the ☑Checkboxes in the adjacent dropdown to choose which specific bank or credit card account(s) the Rule will apply to, e.g., bank fees might always be designated as bank charges.
- **and include the following** allows you to set one or more conditions for the Rule:
- For only one of the conditions to be met select Any or if all of the conditions have to be met select All.
- Set rules based on the downloaded Description or Bank text from the bank, or on the Amount, e.g., your QBO subscription fees may be $56.50 every month.

> ⚠ *Note that creating a Rule based on amount could be an issue if there are other transactions with the same amount. Use amount-based rules with caution.*

- When setting rules QBO has an option to **Then▼** Assign, which means that it will categorize a transaction based on the criteria chosen, or Exclude which will remove the transaction from the banking download without categorizing it.

Once you have set up the conditions for your Rule, you would then choose the details to include on the transaction:

- Transaction type ▼ can be an Expense, Transfer, or Check.

> ✓ *When in doubt, use Expense.*

- **Category▼** represents the account which you will be using that will appear on the Profit and Loss Statement, e.g., QBO subscription fees might use the "dues and subscriptions" category.
- **Payee▼** is the name of the Customer or Supplier selected from the dropdown.

- **Tax▼** is the tax code that you would like to use from the dropdown. With our QBO monthly Expense example, the tax code is HST.
- **Tags**, **Class**, **Location**, and **Memo** are if you would like to assign more information to the rule.
- **Auto-add** toggles ON so you can let QBO automatically add transactions, which means that you will not see them in the review section of the bank download. My personal preference is to toggle this OFF to allow you to review and double check the transaction to which the rules are being applied.

Once done, click on <**Save**>.

Receipts

Receipts are a feature in QBO that allow you to upload copies of actual receipts and bills which QBO then converts to a bill or an expense. This is an advanced topic and beyond the scope of this book.

> ➢ *Receipts generally only works with your home currency. If you have a Bill or Expense in a foreign currency, it will likely not convert the transaction.*

Reconcile Bank and Credit Card Accounts

What Is a Bank Reconciliation?

A bank reconciliation (or bank rec) is a process whereby you ensure that the transactions on your bank statement (the monthly statement that you receive directly from your bank) match the transactions that you have recorded in your accounting. It involves checking each transaction on the bank or credit card statement and ensuring that each appears in your books and vice versa. Any discrepancies between the bank statements and your books must then be resolved.

Why Do You Need a Bank Reconciliation?

A bank reconciliation is essential to ensure that the bank balance in your books is correct and that all transactions that pass through the bank are recorded. The process helps to identify missing transactions, errors and omissions and to ensure that your accounting is accurate and complete. Without a bank reconciliation, it would be very easy to erroneously record or even make up bank transactions, thereby rendering your financial reports inaccurate and, ultimately, meaningless.

Differences between the bank statement and the bank balance often arise due to transactions such as cheques issued, and deposits received, that are still in transit. E.g., when you give someone a cheque, they may take a few days (or months) to cash it. This will be referred to as an "outstanding" transaction on the bank reconciliation and will remain unchecked until the cheque is cashed. This is not an error, but simply a difference that is identified through the process of doing a bank reconciliation.

What Types of Differences Does a Bank Reconciliation Uncover?

There are various types of transactions that a bank reconciliation can uncover, some of which include:

- Outstanding cheques that have not yet been cashed.
- Deposits in transit, i.e., deposits that might be made on the last day of the month but only appear on the next bank statement.
- Bank charges, such as monthly fees, per transaction charges, e-transfer fees, etc., that you only see once you receive your monthly bank statement.
- Interest expenses, such as overdraft interest, credit card interest, and interest on loans that also are not known until the bank statement is received.
- Monthly credit card fees.
- Transactions with incorrect amounts.
- Transactions that have not been entered.
- Transfers between accounts, such as payments to the credit card accounts, loan payments, and withdrawals by the owner/shareholder or repayments.
- Errors made by the bank.

How Often Do You Need to Do a Bank Reconciliation?

Typically, a bank reconciliation is done monthly, since banks send monthly statements. However, these days online banking allows you to retrieve your bank details anytime you want so, if you have numerous transactions, you can also do it more frequently. Some very small businesses do them quarterly or even annually.

How Do You Do a Bank Reconciliation?

This assumes that you have a separate and dedicated bank account for your business, which every business owner should have. However, if you don't have a separate bank account, then a bank reconciliation might simply involve reviewing your business-related bank transactions for the month and ensuring that you have reflected them in QBO.

A bank reconciliation is a straightforward process but requires meticulous attention to detail. Since you are comparing numbers, you need to make sure that each number corresponds exactly.

To do a typical bank reconciliation you need the bank statement that you then compare to the balance in QBO.

A bank reconciliation always starts with the following information from your bank statement:

- Opening balance per the bank statement.
- Closing balance per the bank statement.
- Opening date on the bank statement.
- Closing date on the bank statement.

How Do You Do a Bank Reconciliation in QuickBooks Online?

From the **Left-hand Navigation Bar**, click **Transactions >** and then **[Banking]**. You will notice a **BANK BALANCE** amount and **IN QUICKBOOKS** amount for each account which has been "linked" and is automatically downloading transactions. When all of the downloaded transactions have been entered, these amounts should be identical. If not, it likely means that there are unresolved transactions. The other possible reason for a difference between the **BANK BALANCE** and **IN QUICKBOOKS** amounts is that the latest transactions have not yet been downloaded but the balance has been updated.

To reconcile your account in QBO, click **Accounting >** in the **Left-hand Navigation Bar** and then **[Reconcile]** when the window opens.

The first time you do this, you will see the following screen:

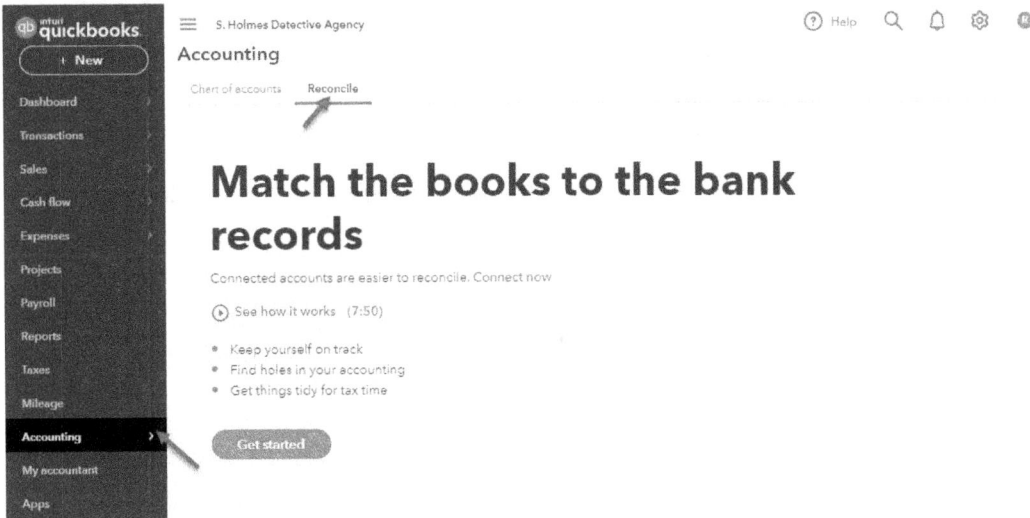

Click on **<Get started>**.

This will bring up the reconciliation interface:

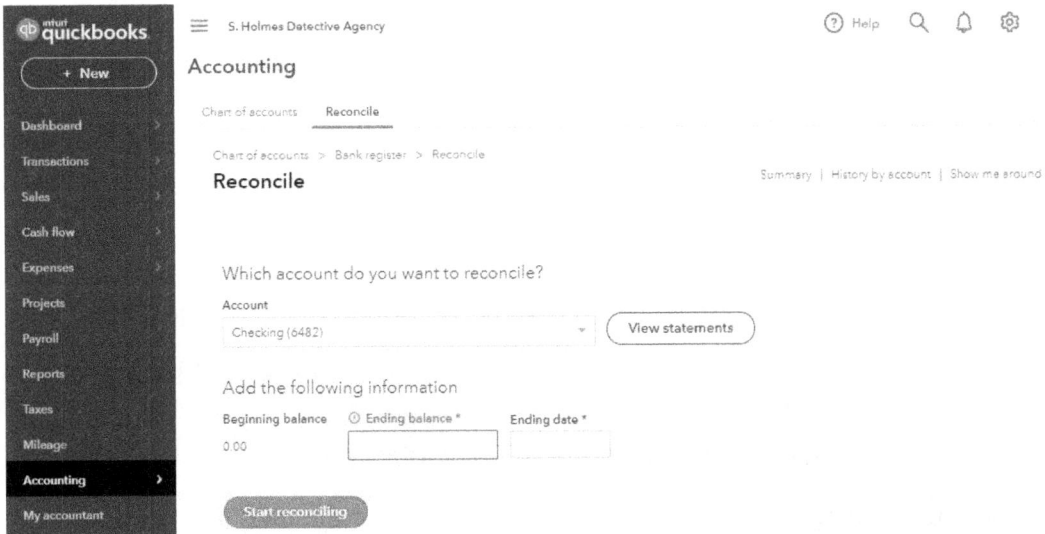

- **Which account do you want to reconcile?** indicates that you should use **Account ▼** to select from all your bank and credit card accounts as well as other asset and liability accounts. Choose the account that you would like to reconcile.
- **Beginning balance** is the opening balance from your bank statement and is automatically entered by QBO since it represents the balance from your last

bank reconciliation. If this is the first time doing a bank reconciliation, this balance will be $0.00.

- **Ending balance*** is the ending balance from your bank statement. You would enter that amount here.
- **Ending date*** is the closing date on your bank statement.

Once you have entered the information above, click on <**Start reconciling**>.

You will then be taken to the following screen:

Most of the transactions are checked automatically. This is because they were entered through the banking interface, so QBO automatically reconciles them.

However, you will note that two transactions that are not checked. These transactions need to be investigated to determine why they have not yet appeared on the bank statement. Some of the possible reasons include:

- Outstanding cheques that have not yet been cashed. Nothing needs to be done, unless they are very old in which case they should be written off.
- Duplicate deposits or payments. The solution to this is to determine why these were entered twice and ensure that the correct one is selected and properly applied to the Invoice or Bill while the duplicate is removed.
- Transfers to and from other accounts that are duplicated. These should be reviewed in the same way as above.

- Multicurrency transfers that use the QBO rate instead of the bank rate. In this case, you can simply change the rate on the transaction to match the bank rate.
- Differences in payment or deposit amounts (often by just 1 or 2 cents) that need to be adjusted to match the bank. Alternatively, if the discrepancies are very small you can enter them as bank charges.

Once everything matches and any differences have been resolved, click on the down arrow on <**Finish Now | ▼** >.

The dropdown has three options:

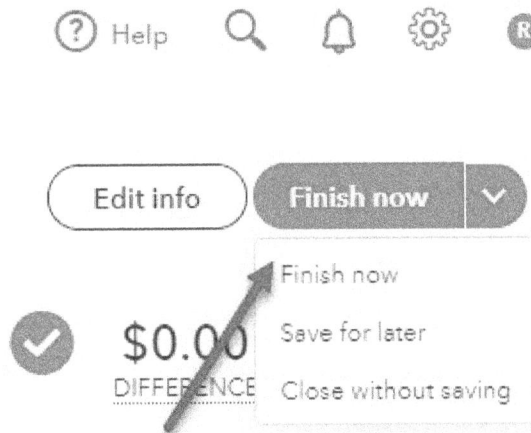

- **Finish now** reflects the reconciliation as having been completed in QBO. Any inadvertent changes in the future, that affect the bank for periods which have been reconciled, can then be easily identified by going to the **History by account** at the top right of the **Accounting: Reconcile** page, which shows you changes to the bank transactions after you have done the reconciliation.
- **Save for later** lets you save the bank rec and come back to it when you are ready.
- **Close without saving** removes any changes you made to the bank rec and closes it without saving. If you choose this option, you will have to re-enter the information.

Doing a regular bank reconciliation is a key accounting function to ensure the integrity of your accounting and reports.

SETTING UP AND WORKING WITH REPORTS

QBO has numerous reports to analyze every facet of your business. The effectiveness of reports depends on the structure that you set up initially, which can then be refined as your business grows.

For the purposes of this book, which is for beginners, we will go over the reports that every new business owner needs to have. I do recommend that you review the available reports and experiment with the different options available. QBO has an almost overwhelming number of different reports and customization options. If you cannot find the exact report that you are looking for, it is very easy to export data into Excel and then customize it as necessary.

Profit and Loss (P&L)

Perhaps the most important and frequently used report for small business owners is the Profit and Loss Statement. This report shows you the overall picture of how your business is doing by showing sales, Cost of Goods Sold, if applicable, Expenses by category, and the amount of profit or loss that your business has generated. The structure of your Profit and Loss Report is informed by the Chart of Accounts so it is important to set up a meaningful Chart of Accounts using guidance from the Chart of Accounts section. This will allow you to capture useful information about your business that allows for effective and insightful analysis.

To generate a Profit and Loss Report, from the **Left-hand Navigation Bar**, click **Reports >**. In the new window, click **[Standard]** and from **Favourites** select **Profit and Loss**.

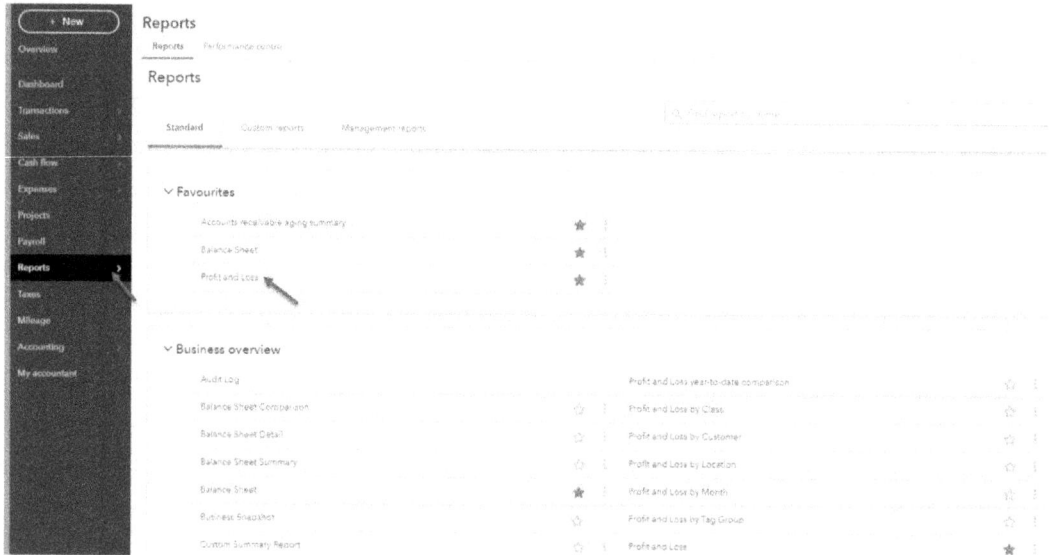

Once you click on **Profit and Loss**, it will bring up the following Report. You then have several options to customize the Report:

- **Report period ▼** lets you select the period for which you would like to see your Profit and Loss Report. This might be for the full fiscal year, last month, this quarter, or any other custom period. The dropdown gives you numerous options for customizing the date.
- **Display columns by ▼** allows you to see the amounts by totals for the period selected, which is the default. Additionally, you can see the breakdown of

the report by months or quarters, Customers, Suppliers, Products/Services, and various other options.

- **Show non-zero or active only ▼** allows you to suppress any categories that are inactive or have $0.00 balances. Alternatively, you can select |All| which shows you all account categories regardless of whether they have any activity during the period selected.
- **Compare another period ▼** (available in Essentials and Plus only) allows you to compare to a prior year or prior period.
- **Accounting method** is cash or accrual as discussed earlier. Usually, you would choose ⊙ **Accrual**.
- **<Run report>** after you have selected your parameters per above. Click on **<Run report>** to refresh or update the report.

> ➤ *Every time you make a change to the report parameters you need to click on*
> *<Run report> to actually update the report and show the changes made.*

- **<Customize>** presents you with a list of options to format and filter your report. You can divide amounts by zero, take out decimals, or show negative amounts in red. It duplicates some of the options discussed above. Filtering is a powerful feature in QBO that allows you to select specific Customers, Suppliers, Products, Classes etc. When a filter is selected, only the transactions relating to the filter will be shown on the report.
- **<Save customization>** allows you to save the parameters that you have selected for the report so that you don't have re-customize every time you want to generate the report. When you have saved a customization, it will show up in **[Custom reports]** on the **Reports** page.

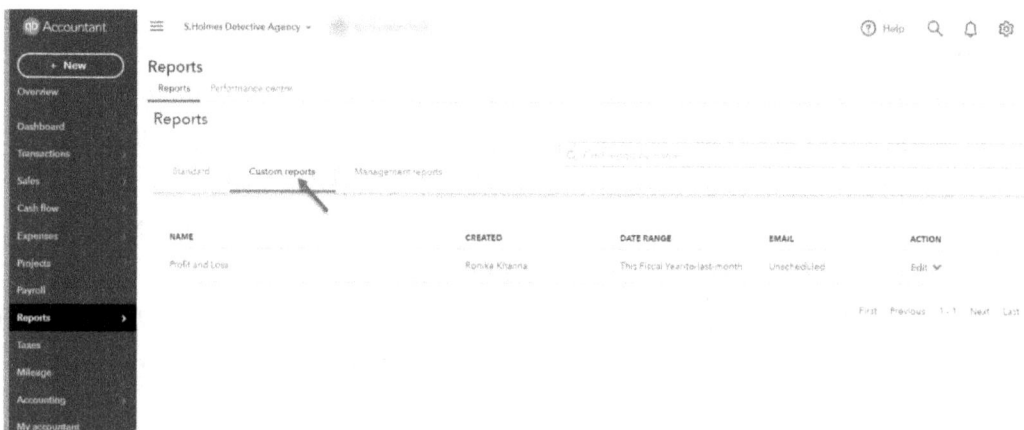

Balance Sheet

The next report that is important for most small businesses and forms part of any business's Financial Statements is the Balance Sheet. This report shows a business's Assets, Liabilities, and Equity. It is where you can see:

- How much money you have in your bank account.
- Total amounts owing from Customers (Accounts Receivable).
- Inventory on hand.
- Investments.
- Fixed assets, such as furniture, equipment, and machinery.
- Total amounts owing to Suppliers (Accounts Payable).
- Loans payable to shareholders.
- Loans payable to third parties.
- Share capital if your business is a corporation which is how much the shareholders have contributed to the company.
- Owner's equity if your business is a sole proprietorship, which is how much the owner has contributed to the company.
- Retained earnings, which is the accumulation of all earnings since inception of the business.

> ➢ *The Total Assets on a Balance Sheet will also be equal to the Total Liabilities and Equity.*

To generate a Balance Sheet, click **Reports** in the **Left-hand Navigation Bar**. On the **Reports** window that opens, click **[Standard]** and then **Balance Sheet** from the **Favourites** section.

Once you click on the **Balance Sheet** you will be presented with all the same options as for **Profit and Loss** above.

Once you have selected the options and **<Run report>**, you can **<Save customization>**, which will then appear in your **[Custom reports]**.

Below is an example of a Balance Sheet for SHDA:

☰ S. Holmes Detective Agency

Balance Sheet Report

‹ Back to report list
Report period

| Custom ▼ | 01/12/2020 | to | 30/06/2021 |

| Display columns by | Show non-zero or active only | Compare another period | Accounting method |
| Total Only ▼ | Active rows/active columns ▼ | Select period ▼ | Cash ● Accrual |

Customize   Save customization

Run report

Collapse Sort ▼ Add notes Edit titles   ✉ 🖶 ↪ ⚙

S. Holmes Detective Agency
Balance Sheet
As of June 30, 2021

	TOTAL
▾ Assets	
▾ Current Assets	
▾ Cash and Cash Equivalent	
Checking (6482)	68,464.66
Total Cash and Cash Equivalent	$68,464.66
▾ Accounts Receivable (A/R)	
Accounts Receivable (A/R)	796.36
Total Accounts Receivable (A/R)	$796.36
Total Current Assets	$69,261.02
▾ Non-current Assets	
Investments	20,000.00
Total Non Current Assets	$20,000.00
Total Assets	$89,261.02
▾ Liabilities and Equity	
▾ Liabilities	
▾ Current Liabilities	
▾ Accounts Payable (A/P)	
Accounts Payable (A/P)	4,746.00
Total Accounts Payable (A/P)	$4,746.00
▾ Credit Card	
Amex Gold	6,361.76
Total Credit Card	$6,361.76
GST/HST Payable	6,347.26
Shareholder Loan	50,000.00
Total Current Liabilities	$67,455.02
Total Liabilities	$67,455.02
▾ Equity	
Retained Earnings	
Profit for the year	21,806.00
Total Equity	$21,806.00
Total Liabilities and Equity	$89,261.02

Accounts Receivable (A/R) Aging Summary

Amounts owing from Customers are summarized on the Accounts Receivable Aging Summary. This is a useful report when you want to see which Customers owe you money, at a glance. You can then drill down on the Report to see details of the Invoices that are still outstanding (not yet paid). Once you identify these, QBO has some tools to help you follow up with Customers, such as Statements and Payment Reminders.

To access the A/R Aging Summary, click **Reports** in the **Left-hand Navigation Bar**. From the **Reports** window that opens, click **[Standard]** and from the **Favourites** section, click on **Accounts receivable aging summary**. You will see the following report:

The options available on the A/R Aging Summary Report are similar to, but more limited than, the Profit and Loss Report. One difference to note is that filters are only available for Customer and Location.

- **Report period ▼** allows you to select a pre-configured date or enter a custom date. A/R Aging Summary Reports are most frequently queried as of the present date; however, you might want to see what you were owed at a previous period for accounting purposes or for additional analysis.
- **Aging method** is specific to aging summaries (both Accounts Receivable and Accounts Payable) and allows you to create divisions in your report by a

specific number of days as well as number of periods that appear on the report. The typical and most common division by **Days per aging period** is 30 days and 4 for **Number of periods**, i.e., you see the total of how much is owing based on 4 30-day increments: 30, 60, 90 and 120 days. This is useful for several reasons:

- It tells you how old your receivables are.
- At a glance you can see the oldest receivables, which will often need the most attention.
- Financial institutions will often assign different weights to older receivables vs younger receivables. For example, if a bank is giving you financing based on the age of your receivable, then younger receivables will have a higher value since older receivables have a lesser likelihood of collection.

Accounts Payable (A/P) Aging Summary

Amounts owing to Suppliers/vendors are summarized on the Accounts Payable
Aging Summary Report. This Report can be accessed by clicking **Reports** in the **Left-
hand Navigation Bar**. In the **Reports** window that opens, scroll down to the **What
you owe** section:

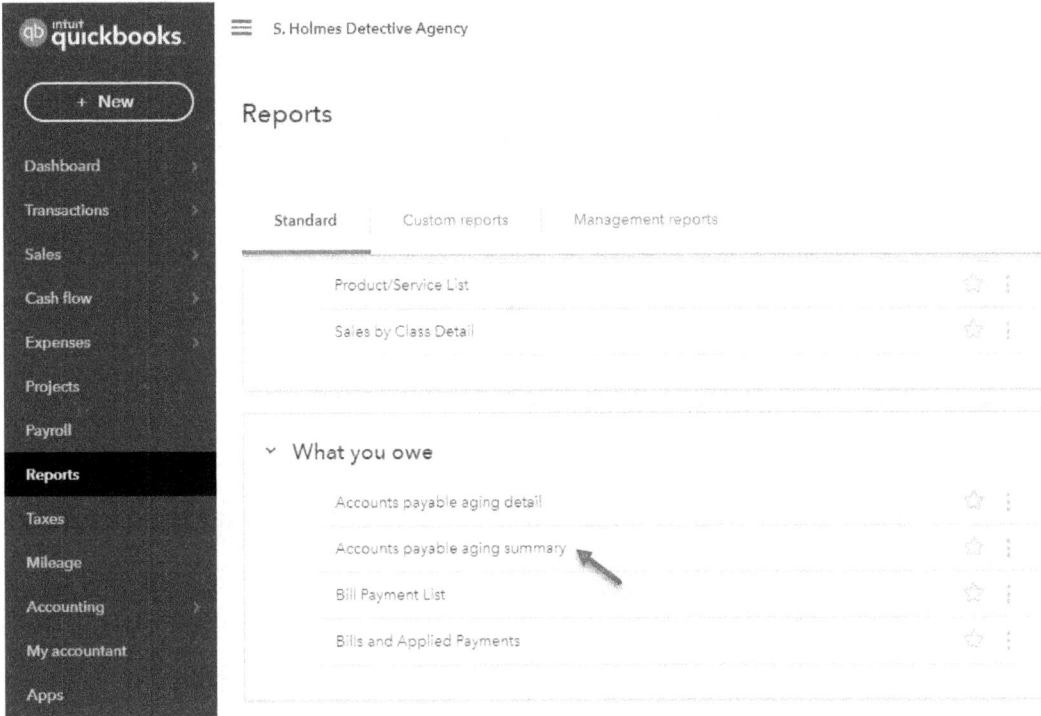

Click on the **Accounts payable aging summary** to open a window for that Report.

The format and available customizations are exactly the same as the Accounts Receivable Aging Summary Report above.

To see the details for each Supplier, click on any of the amounts. This is useful when you want to see exactly what amounts you owe and the dates to which they relate.

Sales by Customer

Being able to see how much you have sold to each Customer provides valuable insights on how much you are selling to each Customer, whether sales have increased or decreased, what types of services they are purchasing, is there a seasonal aspect (i.e., do they purchase more or less during different times of the year), and much more. For the report to be complete and useful, you must enter a customer into the customer field, which depending on how you are entering sales is not always a required field.

To access this and many other sales reports, click **Reports** in the **Left-hand Navigation Bar** and scroll down to the **Sales and customers** section.

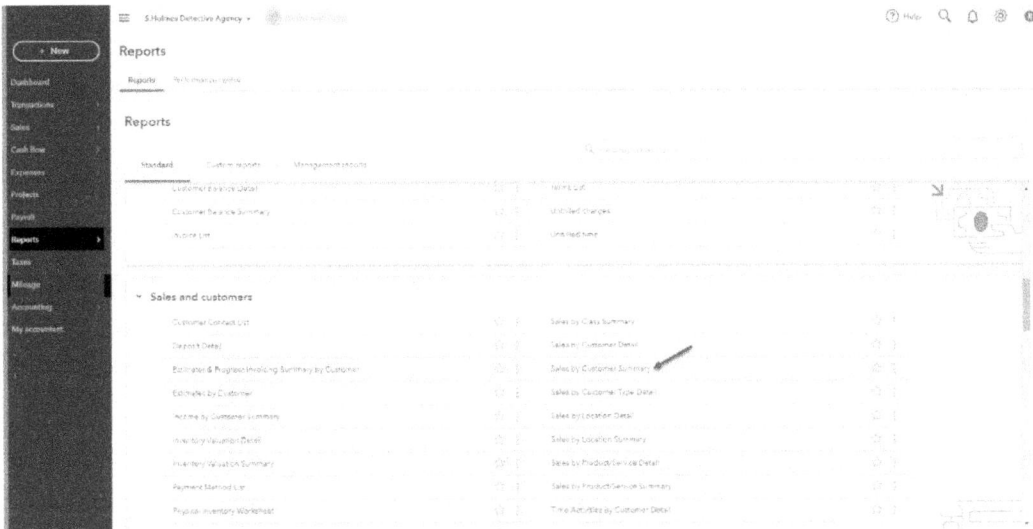

Click **Sales by Customer Summary**, which will open a new window where you can customize the Report with the available options.

❖ Watson would like to compare July's sales to June's, so he has selected:

♦ A **Report period** ▼ of This Month-to-date, which will give him the sales for July.

♦ To compare to June, he selects Previous period under **Compare another period** ▼.

♦ He then clicks on **<Run Report>**.

♦ Since this is a report that he will be looking at monthly, he clicks on **<Save Customization>** which will then save this report in his **[Custom Reports]**.

♦ He can now see that Hooper Inc. and Scarlet Co. have higher sales in July vs June while website sales have gone down. He knows from experience that magnifying glasses, which are mostly sold through their website, are historically low in the summer months as more people are on vacation and not looking at small things.

Expenses by Supplier

As a business owner, you often want to see how much you have paid to your various Suppliers. This Report is similar to Sales by Customer and is available by clicking **Reports** in the **Left-hand Navigation Bar** and scrolling down to the **Expenses and suppliers** list.

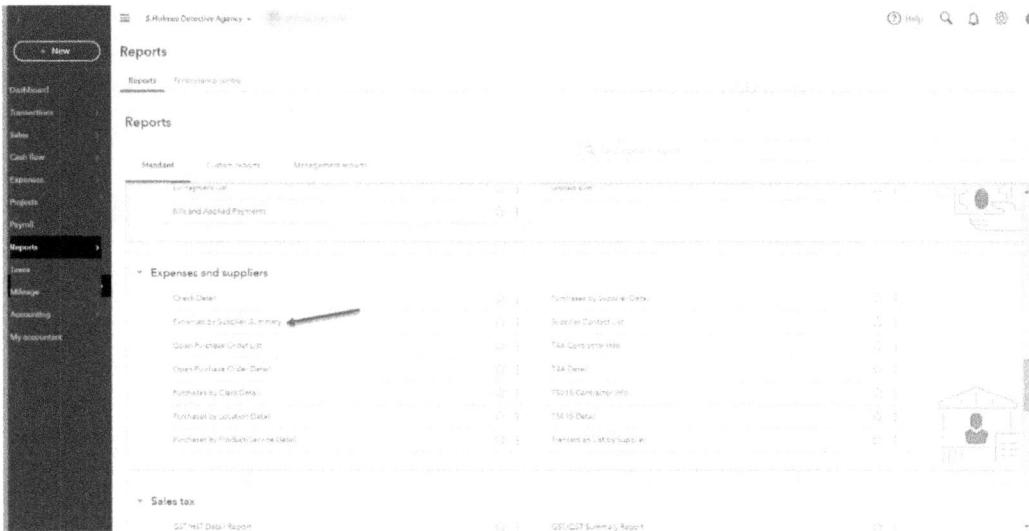

Clicking on **Expenses by Supplier Summary** to bring it up the Report, along with default settings.

❖ *Watson would like to see how much he spent by month for the fiscal year, which starts on December 1st for each supplier. To do this:*

◆ *Under **Report period** ▼, he selects* Custom *and enters the period that he wants to review.*

◆ *Instead of the default, which is* Total*, Watson chooses to **Display columns by** ▼ Months.*

◆ *He then clicks on **<Run Report>**.*

≡ S. Holmes Detective Agency

(?) Help 🔍 🔔 ⚙️

‹ Back to report list
Report period

Customize   Save customization

| Custom | ▼ | 01/12/2020 | to | 30/06/2021 | |

| Display columns by | Show non-zero or active only | Compare another period | Accounting method | |
| Months ▼ | Active rows/active columns ▼ | Select period ▼ | Cash ● Accrual | Run report |

Sort ▼ Add notes

✉ 🖨 ⬆ ⚙️

S. Holmes Detective Agency 🖉

Expenses by Supplier Summary
December 2020 - June 2021

	DEC 2020	JAN 2021	FEB 2021	MAR 2021	APR 2021	MAY 2021	JUN 2021	TOTAL
Amazon Inc		7.12	346.86	244.34	73.90	28.30	84.05	$784.57
Bell							2,289.00	$2,289.00
Butler Assurance							1,580.00	$1,580.00
Cabby Co							3,269.00	$3,269.00
Facebook		70.07	78.29	35.59	47.69	37.16	35.00	$303.80
Hudson Enterprises		104.34	104.34	104.34	107.26	107.26	5,107.26	$5,634.80
Magnussen Electronics					2,700.00		20,000.00	$22,700.00
Ms Irene Adler						1,500.00	7,265.00	$8,765.00
Quickbooks		96.16	96.16	71.73	148.57	148.57	148.57	$709.76
TD				19.00	19.00	19.00	19.00	$76.00
Trilogy		109.23	252.95				865.00	$1,227.18
Wagepoint				7,605.23	7,605.23	7,605.23	7,605.23	$30,420.92
Not Specified		1,589.31	15.04	15.04	69.17	1,145.75	308.57	$3,142.88
TOTAL	$0.00	$1,976.23	$893.64	$8,095.27	$10,770.82	$10,591.27	$48,575.68	$80,902.91

◆ *The report shows all amounts that have been paid to Suppliers since December 1st. Watson has been a little lazy and has not entered Suppliers for all the Expenses that he categorized through the banking download. As such, there are some transactions that are shown as **Not Specified**. He can fix this by clicking on the **Not specified TOTAL** of $3,142.88, which brings up the detail for the account. He can then click on each transaction to edit it and add the payee (Supplier).*

Other Reports

- **Statement of Cash Flows** is an important accounting Report that shows you where your cash is being spent. This is a more advanced Report for purposes of analysis.

- **Open Invoices** shows you each Invoice that has not yet been paid by Customers. This report facilitates following up delinquent payments by looking at each invoice and sending a follow up.

- **Sales by Product/Service Summary** is a useful report that shows you a summary of your sales by products or services. It allows you to analyze how your Products and Services are selling and informs your marketing efforts and pricing strategy.

- **Sales tax** lists several **Summary** and **Detail** Reports that show you all transactions that are included in your GST/HST filings and can be useful to review to ensure that tax codes are properly applied, to see details of the sales tax filing, and in case of audit by CRA (or Revenue Quebec).

- **Trial Balance** is a popular Report for accountants that shows you a summary of each balance at a specified date in the Chart of Accounts. Rather than generating the Balance Sheet and Profit and Loss Report separately to see all your accounts, the Trial Balance shows everything in one Report.

- **General Ledger i**s also frequently requested by accountants and comprises the detailed transactions in each account for a specified period that you would customize under **Report period**. This follows the structure of the Trial Balance and is essentially an expanded version of that Report.

Email, Print, and Export Reports

Every report in QBO has the following icons:

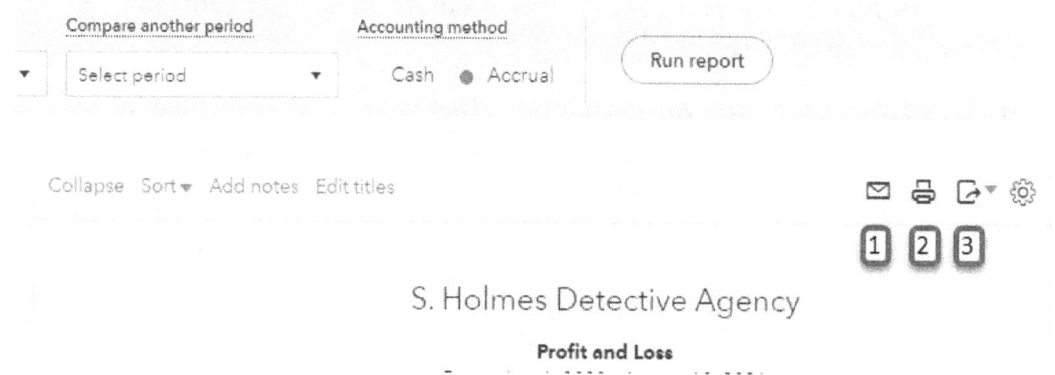

	Compare another period		Accounting method		
▼	Select period	▼	Cash ● Accrual		Run report

Collapse Sort ▼ Add notes Edit titles   ✉ 🖨 ↗▼ ⚙

                                                          [1] [2] [3]

S. Holmes Detective Agency

Profit and Loss

1.   ✉ **Email icon** brings up a dialog box from where you can enter the email address of a recipient, CC, Subject line and a Body for the message. You can then rename the Report if necessary. QBO then sends an email to the recipient(s) along with the Report in PDF format.

Email Report

To

ronika@montrealfinancial.ca

CC

Subject

Your Profit and Loss Report

Body

Hello

Attached is the Profit and Loss report for S. Holmes Detective Agency.

Regards
Ronika Khanna

Report

Profit and Loss Report   .pdf

Cancel   Send

2.   ⎙ **Print icon** brings up a print dialog box that allows you to adjust the
      parameters and either print the report or save it as a PDF.

3.   ↪ **Export icon** will export the Report to Excel or PDF, which will create the
      file and download it directly to your computer (usually found in the
      Downloads folder depending on your computer settings). The ability to
      export to Excel allows for extensive analysis, especially if you have some skill
      with Excel, as you can sort and format your data, and, if you're feeling
      ambitious, create Pivot Tables, sub-totals and v-lookups to query your data.

SET UP RECURRING TRANSACTIONS

A recurring transaction, as mentioned earlier, is an automation whereby QBO will enter the same or similar transactions on a date specified by you. Recurring transactions are particularly useful in the following situations:

- If you charge rent every month to one or more tenants.
- If you pay rent every month to a landlord.
- For membership or subscription businesses where your Customers pay you the same amount on a periodic basis.
- For subscriptions that you pay that are the same from month to month (or period to period).
- Monthly or periodic retainers, such as those charged by law or accounting firms.
- Monthly lease or financing payments.
- Transactions that occur frequently that are not necessarily set up as recurring but simply as a template that can be used when needed.
- A monthly accrual for an amount that you only pay once a year.
- A monthly transfer such as payment of a loan.

When setting up a recurring transaction, you have two choices:

1. You can set up a new transaction that you want to be recurring.
2. You can make an existing transaction recurring.

Setting Up a New Recurring Transaction

The example we will use to illustrate a New Recurring Transaction is as follows:

❖ *Dr. Watson would like to pay a new Supplier, the Irregulars and Co., a fixed monthly amount of $750.00 for their investigative work. He doesn't want to have to enter this every month in QBO. He has also set up an automatic payment directly through his bank account that goes out on the 5th of each month.*

◆ *To do this, he goes to the ⚙ **Gear icon** and clicks on **Recurring transactions** under **LISTS**. In the new window, he then clicks <New>.*

◆ *He sees the following pop-up, which asks him to select a **Transaction Type ▼**. In this case he will be setting up a monthly* Bill *to reflect the Expense:*

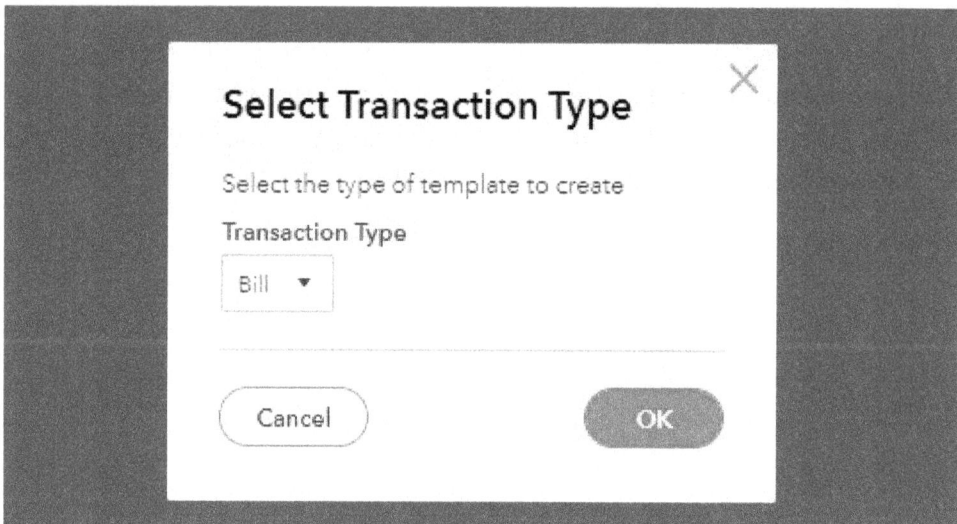

Select Transaction Type

Select the type of template to create

Transaction Type

Bill ▼

Cancel OK

◆ *He clicks <OK> to open the next window.*

> ❖ *He enters the details so that the Bill is entered automatically on the 5th day of every month:*

- **Template name** should be descriptive so that when you see your list of recurring transactions you know exactly what it relates to
- **Interval▼** can be daily, monthly, weekly or yearly. You can also do bimonthly or quarterly by entering the number of months, e.g., bimonthly would be 2 months while quarterly would be every 3 months.
- **Day▼** can be a specified date, or you can choose the last day of the month.
- **Start date** is always a date in the future when you want QBO to start creating the transaction. If you put today's date, then it will follow the instructions to create the first Bill on the fifth day of next month.

> ➢ *You can create a recurring Bill today to start at any date in the future.*

- **End▼** allows you enter the last date on which a recurring series of Bills should be entered after which QBO will cease to enter the Bills automatically. This is useful when you have a fixed term after which the contract ends or has to be renewed.
- All other fields are similar to entering a Bill as explained in the section on creating Bills.

Once you have created the recurring Bill to your satisfaction, you would click on
<Save template>. The Bill will be created and show up in the list of recurring
transactions.

Once the recurring template has been created, there are several different options
available in the dropdown under the **ACTION** button at the right-hand side next to
the template:

CUSTOMER/SUPPLIER	AMOUNT	ACTION
Quickbooks	68.99	Edit ▼
Irregulars and Co.	847.50	Use
		Duplicate
		Pause
		Skip next date
		Delete

- Use is very useful if you want to enter the transaction right away. Clicking
  on it will create a new transaction immediately, which you can then edit and
  then save as a new transaction.
- Duplicate allows you to duplicate the template for another supplier or
  vendor that might be similar.
- Pause lets you stop the automatic entry of the transaction for a specified
  period of time in cases when you will not be paying your supplier for a few
  months.
- Skip next date will simply not enter the next scheduled transaction.
- Delete allows you to delete the Recurring Transaction when you no longer
  need it.

Setting Up a Recurring Transaction Based on an Existing Transaction

You can also create a recurring transaction directly from an existing transaction.

❖   *Watson wants to set up a monthly retainer transaction from Scotland Yard. He has already entered the Invoice for July and wants to set it up for September since he and Mr. Holmes take the full month of August off and therefore do not invoice.*

◆   *To enter the transaction, Watson simply goes to **Sales > (or Invoicing >)** on the **Left-hand Navigation Bar** and selects **[Customers]** in the new window. He then clicks on "Scotland Yard" and finds the Invoice that he wants to set up as recurring. He opens up the Invoice and clicks on **Make recurring** at the bottom.*

◆   *The **Recurring Bill** template opens up and he follows the instruction from above for creating a Recurring Transaction.*

QBO automatically assigns a **Template name** which is the name of the Customer; however, this can be changed to be more specific.

FILING YOUR SALES TAX RETURN

Once you set up sales tax, QBO will track the sales tax that you collect from Customers and the sales tax that you pay on Expenses based on the tax code that you assign to each transaction. There is a separate section in QBO where you can see the accumulation of all the sales tax transactions, and "file" a Sales Tax Return that then clears out the transactions for the specified period, making way for the Sales Tax Return for the next period. The purpose of this feature is to ensure that your Sales Tax Returns are accurately reflected in QBO, review any issues, and close a sales tax period so that any transactions entered after a Sales Tax Return has been filed are then carried over to the next filing period.

> ➤ *A typical GST/HST Report has various fields. For most businesses, there are only 5 fields and 3 calculations that need to be completed, which we will discuss in greater detail as we go over the Report.*

The process for filing a Sales Tax Return in QBO is as follows:

1. Click on **Taxes** from the **Left-hand Navigation Bar**. You will see the following interface:

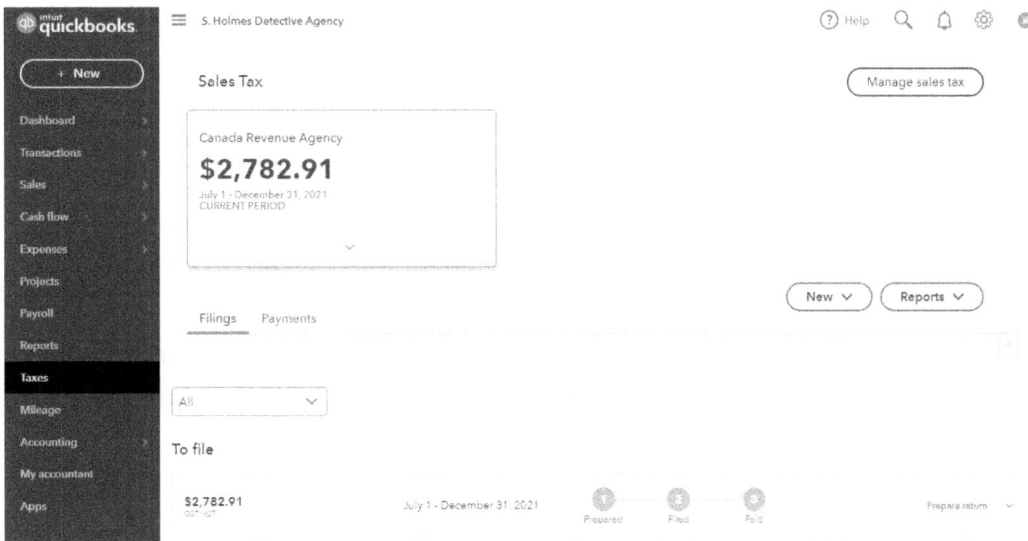

2. Click **Prepare return** ▼ at the bottom right.

3. The next screen shows you a GST/HST return with all the fields that you need to file the actual GST/HST return:

- **Filing period ▼** represents the period for which the Sales Tax Return is due. This might be annual/yearly, quarterly, or monthly as discussed above. Alternatively, you can enter custom dates.
- **Start date** is the starting date of the period. This might be January 1st or the first day of your fiscal year if you are a corporation, or the start of the quarter or month, depending on your filing frequency.
- **End date** is the last date of the period that corresponds to your filing frequency.
- **Filing date** is the date on which you are filing the Sales Tax Return with CRA. This is also the date on which the transaction for the sales tax filing is automatically entered by QBO.

4. Once you have entered the dates, the sales tax owing (or refund receivable) will be updated in QBO to reflect the period selected. This should agree to the amount on the Balance Sheet at this date.

5. A typical GST/HST report has 4 fields that must be completed:

   - **Sales and other revenue – Line 101** represents your total taxable sales.
   - Total GST/HST and adjustments for period – Line 105 represents the GST/HST collected on Sales.
   - Input Tax Credits (ITCs) – Line 106/Total ITCs and Adjustments – Line 108 represents the GST/HST paid on Expenses.
   - **Balance – Line 113** shows the net GST/HST payable or refundable (this is obtained by deducting **Line 108** from **Line 105**).

   All other fields relate to more advanced GST/HST returns and are generally not applicable to regular small businesses.

6. Once you have completed the return in QBO, click on **Print** to either print it or preferably save it as a PDF in your accounting folder on your computer. You will need this to file your actual GST/HST Return with CRA.

7. You can then click on **<Mark as filed>**. Doing this will "file" the return in QBO, create the Journal Entry that posts the GST/HST payable or refund to an account called "GST/HST suspense". Any adjustments to previous periods made after this date will be tracked by QBO and reflected on your next Report. Once you have clicked on **<Mark as filed>** you will see the message below. Click **<Continue>** to be taken back to the main Sales Tax interface.

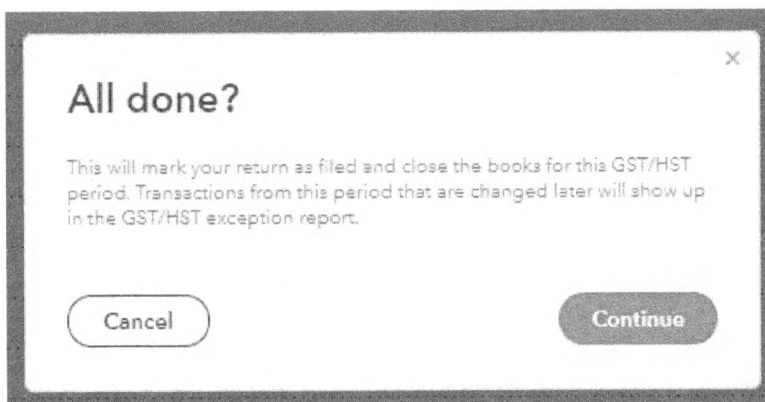

All done?

This will mark your return as filed and close the books for this GST/HST period. Transactions from this period that are changed later will show up in the GST/HST exception report.

Cancel   Continue

8. The amounts from the printed Return that you saved as a PDF or printed in Step 6 should then be transcribed on the Return to be filed with CRA.

✓ *After registering for GST/HST, you will receive a letter from CRA indicating the date of registration, your GST/HST number, and the filing frequency. If you are unsure, you can refer to this letter. This is usually also available online through* CRA My Business Account*.*

➤ *A GST/HST return can be submitted to CRA in the following three ways:*

1. *By completing the paper form that you receive in the mail and enclosing it with a cheque for any amounts payable.*
2. *By using GST/HST Netfile through CRA My business account and making payment through online banking.*
3. *By submitting the full return using the business tax filing service available at most banks.*

Additional Sales Tax Options and Relevant Reports

Once you have filed your Return, there are several options available from the
dropdown at **Record payment| ▼** :

- **Record payment** is where you would record the payment that you have
  made to CRA.
- **Record refund** is the same as **Record Payment** except for a refund.
- **View summary** shows you the summary of the Report that was filed in this
  period.
- **View GST/HST detail** shows you the details of the Report and each
  transaction that makes up the totals on the summary Report.
- **View exception details** is a Report that shows you any changes that have
  been made to a period that was already filed. Since filing a Report closes the
  period, any changes to sales tax for a prior "filed" period will show up on a
  future Report.
- **Undo filing** is a handy feature that allows you to reverse a filing that has
  already been done. This might be necessary if you have made an error or

forgotten to include some transactions. This should only be done before filing the report with CRA. Otherwise, any changes should be dealt with in a future period. It should also be noted that, if you have exceptions in a current period filing, QBO's $\boxed{\text{Undo filing}}$ feature does not properly deal with these, so be very careful when using this feature.

Other Sales Tax Reports

QBO provides several sales tax summary and detail Reports, some of which were discussed above, that are useful when you want to see the breakdown of what you have claimed on your summary Report and in the case of audit by CRA (or Revenue Quebec).

All the reports discussed above are also available in the Reports section. You would click on the **Reports >** from the **Left-hand Navigation Bar**. In the **Reports** interface that opens, scroll down to the **Sales Tax** section as seen in the screenshot below:

Other available reports include:

- **Taxable Sales Summary**, which shows you all sales that are subject to sales tax and the breakdown of sales and GST/HST.
- **Transaction Detail by Tax Code** shows you the breakdown of the Report by tax code, e.g., each taxable transaction that is subject to GST or HST Ontario or HST in another province. This is especially useful in the case of audits or to review transactions to ensure that transactions have the correct tax codes.
- **Transactions without sales tax** shows you all transactions on which no tax code was entered and can be used to ensure that there are no errors or omissions.

WHAT ARE JOURNAL ENTRIES?

Without taking you through an accounting seminar, suffice it to say that a Journal Entry is a way to record a transaction when the transaction is somewhat unspecific, outside of the normal course of operations, or in the interest of time and efficiency.

To better understand this, let's identify transaction types that are NOT Journal Entries in QBO:

- A Sale transaction is entered through **Sales >** (or **Invoicing >**) in the **Left-hand Navigation Bar**.
- An Expense transaction is entered through **Expenses >**.
- A bank transaction is entered through **Transactions >** (or **Banking >**).
- Payroll is entered through **Payroll** in the **Left-hand Navigation Bar**.

A Journal Entry is often used for transactions that happen only occasionally and as such there isn't a separate designated journal for them (such as Sales or Expenses). Accountants also use Journal Entries to enter year-end adjustments or to combine a series of transactions, which can be a bit more complicated. A Journal Entry always has an equal number of debits and credits.

How to Record a Journal Entry

To create a Journal Entry in QBO, click on the **<+ New>** button and select **Journal entry** under **OTHER** to bring up the screen for the Journal Entry.

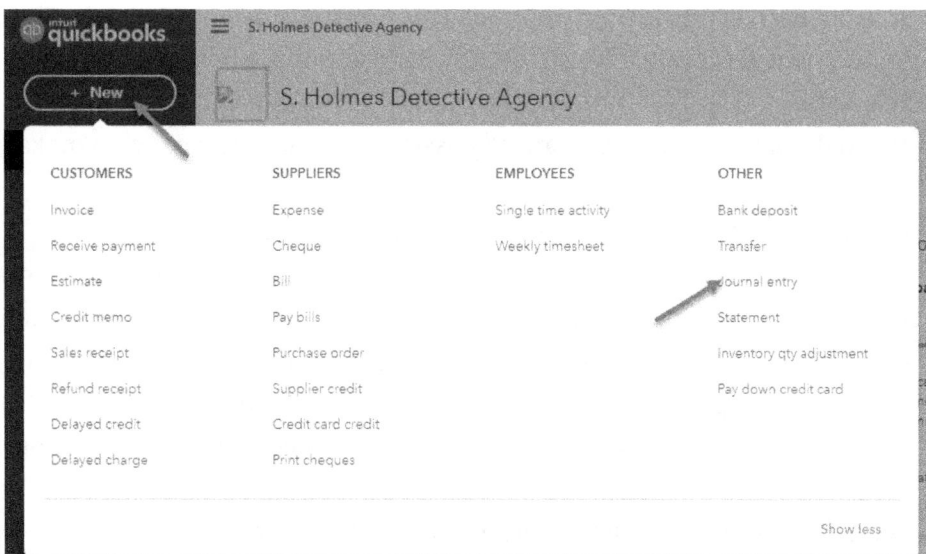

❖ *Watson knows that he will be receiving a Bill from the lawyer for SHDA at the end of July. Although he doesn't know the exact amount, he has an approximation. He wants to enter this to ensure that the Profit and Loss Report for the period, that he is going to present to Mr. Holmes, reflects this Expense. He Estimates the Bill will be about $5,000.00.*

◆ *He enters the following Journal Entry to reflect the estimated Expense:*

🕓 **Journal Entry no.7**   ⚙ ⑦ Help ✕

Journal date	Journal no.
31/07/2021	7

#	ACCOUNT	DEBITS	CREDITS	DESCRIPTION	NAME	SALES TAX
1	Legal and professional fees	5,000.00		Reflect estimated lawyer fees	Moran and Associates	
2	Accrued Expenses		5,000.00	Reflect estimated lawyer fees		

| | Total | 5,000.00 | 5,000.00 | | | |

Add lines   Clear all lines

Memo

📎 Attachments   Maximum size: 20MB

Cancel	Clear		Make recurring		Save	Save and new ▾

- **Journal date** is the date of the transaction that will appear in QBO. Since he knows he will receive a Bill dated July 31st, sometime in August, Watson uses this date.
- **Journal no.** is usually automatically assigned but can be edited to make it descriptive.
- **ACCOUNT** is the Expense category from the Chart of Accounts.
- **DEBITS** are the amounts to be debited. This is a somewhat complex area of accounting; however, it is enough to know that Expenses are always debits.
- **CREDITS** are entered to balance the corresponding debit. Since the legal fees will be payable to the lawyers, Watson has set up a current liability account called "Accrued Expenses", which is the accounting terminology for unspecific amounts payable.
- **DESCRIPTION** lets us know what the transaction relates to.

- **NAME** is the name of the Supplier or Customer.
- **SALES TAX** can be added here. However, since this is simply an estimate and no Bill has been received, sales tax is not applicable.

◆ *Once Watson has entered the data in the various fields, he clicks on **<Save>** to enter the transaction in the books.*

Common Transactions that Use Journal Entries

Shareholder Loans (Payable and Receivable)

Shareholder Loans Payable, i.e., money that the company owes to one or more shareholders, arises when the shareholder either:

a) loans money to the company,

b) transfers assets like computers, inventory, or other assets to the business, or

c) incurs Expenses or is paid a dividend or a salary but the Shareholder chooses to leave the funds that they should have received (as net salary or dividends) in the company to be repaid at a later date.

The best way to record this is as follows:

Set up a new account in the Chart of Accounts called "shareholder loan". The account type in QBO is current liability account (on the Balance Sheet) while the detail type is short term borrowings from related parties.

If the funds have come into the bank account from the shareholder, it can simply be allocated as a deposit or a transfer to the shareholder account (no Journal Entry necessary). A deposit is a little more flexible than a transfer as you can show the name of the shareholder but otherwise a deposit and a transfer, in this case, are functionally the same.

If a shareholder is transferring assets to the corporation, you would record the following Journal Entry:

The Journal Entry for dividends paid (that are reflected on a T5/RL3) for the year and are reinvested into the company would be shown as:

A shareholder might want to take a nominal amount of dividends during the year to smooth out tax owing in future years, but then reinvest them in the company.

Shareholder loan receivable i.e., the shareholder owing the company money is a more common situation and usually occurs when the shareholder withdraws funds from the company which they might later either take as a dividend or repay to the company.

Use the shareholder loan account created per instructions above. Even though this is technically a liability account it is better to have one shareholder loan account where all transactions can be offset against each other. If there is a shareholder loan receivable by the corporation from the shareholder, there will be negative liability.

Shareholder loan accounts only apply to corporations. Sole proprietorships would have an owner's equity account which would be set up as an equity account rather than a liability. In this case dividends are not applicable.

The payment from the bank account would be categorized as an Expense or a transfer to the shareholder loan account.

Corporate Tax Expense, Payments, and Interest/Penalties

If your business is profitable, you usually have to pay corporate taxes at the end of the year. Additionally, depending on the amount of corporate tax, you might also have to pay quarterly or monthly tax instalments. If payments are made after certain due dates, interest and/or penalties on corporate income tax might also apply.

Although there are complex rules under GAAP for how to calculate and reflect income taxes, most companies can usually record the amount payable and corresponding expense as determined on their tax return.

To record corporate income taxes, two new accounts should be created in your Chart of Accounts:

- "Income tax expense", which is an Expense account (I like to use "other expense" for this account type so that it shows under all other Expenses on the Profit and Loss Statement).
- "Income tax payable", which is a current liability account.

The corporate tax expense from the tax return is simply recorded as a Journal Entry on the year end date of the corporation as follows:

- Debit: Income tax expense
- Credit: Income tax payable

When payment of the corporate income taxes is made, generally several months after the year end, do the following:

From the banking download in QBO, categorize the payment as a payment/expense to income tax payable (remember you have already set up the Expense so you don't want to duplicate it) and indicate the name of the revenue agency to whom it is being paid

If the payment amount exceeds the Expense amount due to interest and/or penalties, you would "split" the transaction in the banking download, create a new Expense account for "interest and penalties" and categorize the appropriate amounts to the interest and penalties account, while the balance is allocated to income tax payable. This will clear out the income tax liability account if the full amount of the balance is paid.

When making payment of the corporate tax payable:

- Debit: income tax payable (reduce the liability)
- Debit: interest and penalties (if applicable)
- Credit: bank account from which the payment is made (for the full amount of the payment)

Home Office Expenses:

Shareholders who are also employees of corporations and owners of sole proprietorships may be entitled to a home office expense deduction under certain circumstances. If you qualify:

1. Create a spreadsheet that list 100% of the following home office Expenses for the year including:

- Rent
- Condo fees
- Interest portion of the mortgage payable
- Utilities
- Property and School Taxes
- Insurance
- Property maintenance (e.g., cleaning staff or gardener)
- Repairs to the whole property
- Telephone
- Internet

2. On the spreadsheet indicate the percentage of the home that relates to the home office portion only and multiply by the total amount above to get the home office Expense for each category
3. Set up each category above in the chart of account as an Expense. Each category can also be listed as a sub-category of home office Expenses for further clarity.

4. Create a Journal Entry as follows:

- Debit: Rent, Condo fees, Insurance etc. (each category on a separate line with the corresponding amount that relates to the home office. This can all be one Journal Entry.)
- Credit: Shareholder Loan (the exact total of home office Expenses can then be paid out to the shareholder).

Depreciation Expense and Accumulated Depreciation

Certain high value purchases of assets, that have a useful life beyond one year, like computers, printers, cell phones, furniture, photography equipment, machinery, etc. are recorded as capital assets (property, plant, and equipment) on the Balance Sheet rather than asExpenses on the Profit and Loss Report. They are then depreciated over time using one of several methods. The method to calculate depreciation used by Revenue Canada (CRA) is the declining balance method. Each asset is assigned to a specific CCA (capital cost allowance) class that has a pre-determined rate. For example, computers and related purchases are Class 50 with a 55% depreciation rate, while furniture and photography equipment would be Class 8 with a 20% depreciation rate.

The depreciation calculation is based on the Undepreciated Capital Cost, which is the cost of the assets less any depreciation taken in prior years. In the first year, the half year rule is applied, which means that only 50% of the depreciation is allowed. See an example of how CCA is calculated:

Cost of Car	25,000.00
HST Rate Ontario	13%
Total HST	**3,250.00**
Business use of car	75.00%
CCA Rate in Class 10	30.00%
Half Year Rule in Year 1	50.00%
CCA Claimable in Year 1 (Cost Only)	2,812.50
HST Calculator	13/113
HST Claimable	373.89

Note that other methods of depreciation can be taken for the purpose of Financial Statements, including straight line or units of production if this gives a more accurate view of the usage of the asset.

To record the Journal Entry in QBO:

1. Set up an account for depreciation Expense. You can either set up an account for each category of asset, e.g., depreciation computer equipment, depreciation furniture etc. OR you can set up one combined Expense account.

> ➢ *QBO has this as an "Other expense" when scrolling through detail type, however, it might make more sense to show this an "expense" since it is part of operating Expenses. For detail type, you can use other general/administrative Expense*

2. You would then create accounts for accumulated depreciation for each asset. This allows you to monitor the depreciated value of each asset. The accumulated depreciation asset account is a "contra" account since it will always have a negative balance while assets are usually positive. The account in QBO would be created as a "property, plant and equipment" account where you would selected accumulated depreciation as the detail type. When name the account it is common practice to call it accumulated depreciation (depn) – computer or furniture etc. depending on the category of asset to which it applies.

3. Enter the Journal Entry for depreciation as follows:

   * Debit: Depreciation Expense
   * Credit: Accumulated Depreciation

Recording a Journal Entry, while usually under the purview of accountants, can also be done by business owners and support staff, particularly for simple transactions like the ones listed above.

APPENDIX: ARE YOU TRANSFERRING EXISTING DATA?

If you are a brand-new business, you would simply follow the instructions in this guide to set up your business in QBO. If, however, you already have data either in a spreadsheet, QuickBooks Desktop, or another accounting software, you will have to make a decision as to how to transfer the data so you can use it in QBO.

Importing Your Data from QuickBooks Desktop

QBO has made it relatively straightforward to import your data from QuickBooks Desktop (QBDT). To migrate your data:

1. Create a new file in QBO, following the steps in signing up for the first time.
2. Go to the **Company** menu in QBDT.

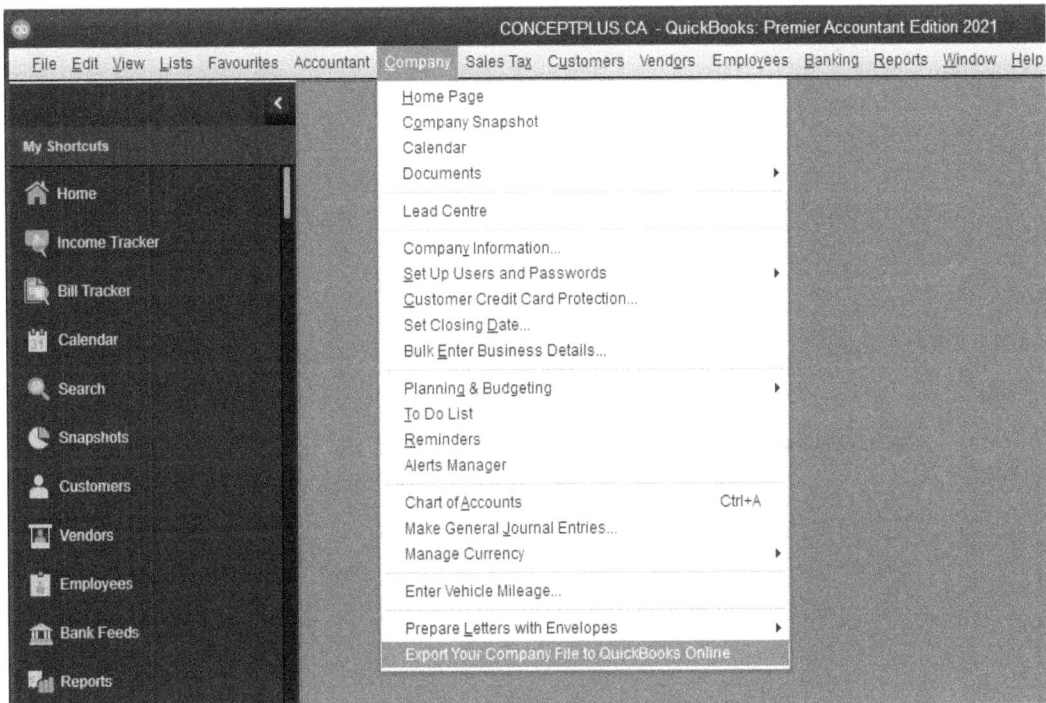

3. Click on Export Your Company File to QuickBooks Online.

4. You will be taken to the following screen:

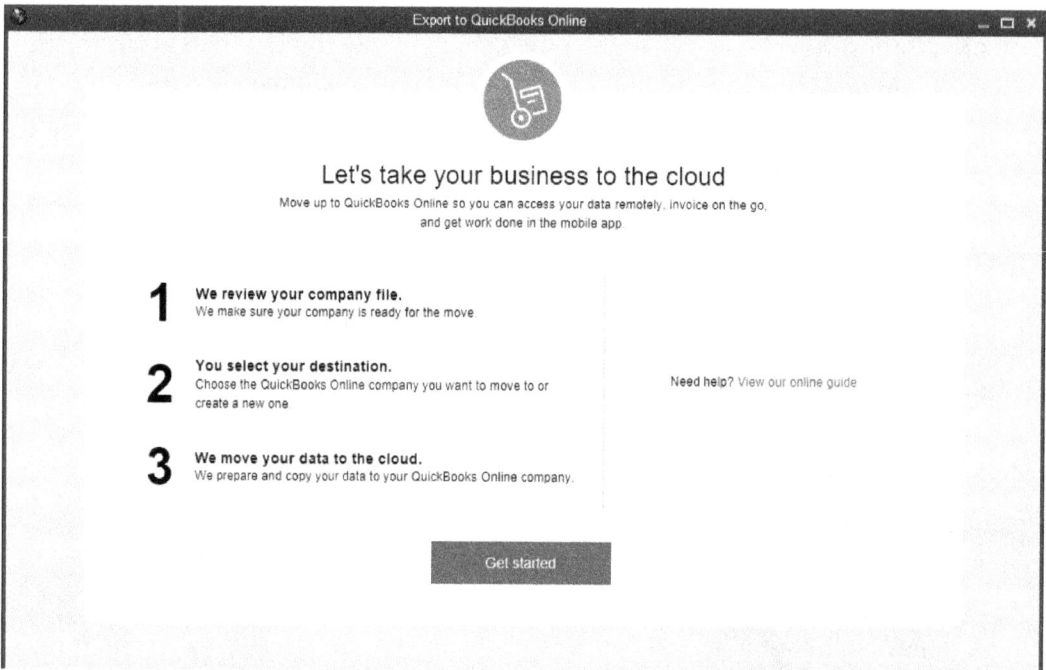

5. Click on **<Get started>** to start a quick review of your QBDT file.
6. If all is ok, you will see the following screen:

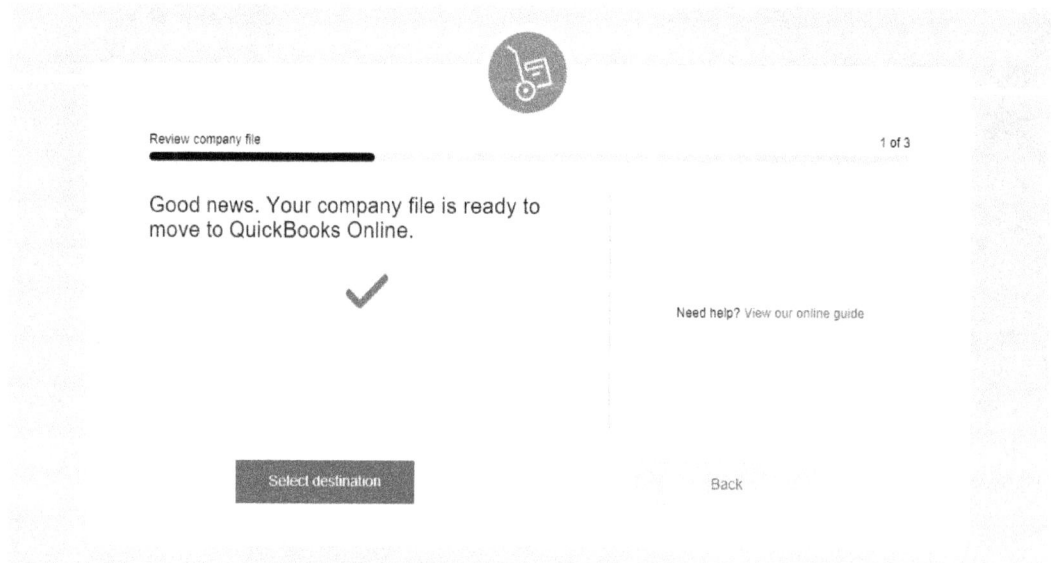

7. Click on <Select destination>.

8. The next screen asks you for the login and password for your QBO account, which you set up per instructions in Signing Up For The First Time.

9. Click on **\<Sign in\>**.

10. You will then be taken to the next screen. **Select a company** ▼ will show the company you have just set up in QBO.

Select your destination   2 of 3

Select your destination

Choose the company in which to import your desktop file. Your desktop data
will replace—not merge with— the data in the online company you choose.

Select a company

S. Holmes Detective Agency   ▼

Don't see your company in the list?

| Continue | Cancel |

11. **Select your destination** by ensuring that your business name is showing in **Select a company** ▼, and click on **<Continue>**.
12. The transition from QBDT to QBO will overwrite ALL data that is currently in your QBO file. This is fine assuming you have not yet entered anything into your new QBO file.

Select your destination   2 of 3

Do you want us to replace all of your
Concept Plus Inc. QuickBooks Online data
with your QuickBooks Desktop data?

If you want to proceed with overwriting the data in this company, please
type the word AGREE below.

                                                        Need help? View our online guide

    AGREE

| Replace | Back |

13. Type "AGREE" in the box.
14. Click on **<Replace>**.
15. You will then see the following two screens letting you know that the data is being imported:

Preparing data to export to the QuickBooks Online file.

87 %

Move data   3 of 3

We're getting your data ready for the cloud

Please keep QuickBooks Desktop running during this step. It can take up to 30 minutes.

Retrieving you transactions.

Syncing any payroll data.   Need help? View our online guide

Preparing your file for move.

We're moving your data to the cloud

We're transferring your data now. When it's done, we'll send a confirmation email with a summary report to

ronika@montrealfinancial.ca

Need help? View our online guide

To check out QuickBooks Online, take a tour

Got it

16. Once your data has been imported into QBO, you will receive an email letting you know that the process is complete.

> ➢ *If you receive an email telling you that they were unable to complete the transfer, you should contact QBO customer support as they should in most cases be able to help you troubleshoot any errors.*

Transferring Data from Another Accounting Software or Spreadsheet

A small business might decide to transition to QBO for a variety of reasons:

- You are currently using spreadsheets which have become difficult to manage.
- Your spreadsheets do not provide the data that you require to properly analyze your business.
- Your current accounting system is too technical and/or not user friendly.
- Your current accounting system does not have the features that you require.
- You want to be able to access your data online rather than through your desktop.

If you already have a business and the accounting data is in another software or spreadsheet, then you the easiest thing to do is to transfer ending balances and lists which include the Chart of Accounts, Customers, and Suppliers. This is the method we will explore below.

> ➢ *Alternatively, you can transfer all the individual transactions from your existing software or spreadsheet. Note that this is a technical and complex process that should be undertaken by someone with a strong accounting and QBO foundation. It is also beyond the scope of this book.*

Transfer Ending Balances

Why You Need Ending Balances

When transitioning from a different accounting system to QBO, whether it is a spreadsheet or another accounting software, one of the first steps is to ensure that your data at the previous year end for your business is correctly reflected and to establish continuity. This is done by transferring the balances from your Balance

Sheet at a specific date, which is ideally the year end date of your business. The amounts on a Balance Sheet are essentially an accumulation of all activity since inception of your business and broadly includes assets, liabilities, and equity.

How To Enter Opening Balances

In accounting, a Balance Sheet is structured so that the assets ALWAYS equal the liabilities and equity. This is achieved through the magic of debits and credits where every debit has a corresponding credit (there can be more than one credit or debit in a transaction as you will see below). Consequently, when opening balances are entered there should be no discrepancies between the debits and credits.

> ➢ *There are two methods to enter opening balances in QBO:*
>
> ⇨ ***Enter opening balances directly through the Chart of Accounts****: The first way is to enter the opening balance directly into each account on the Chart of Accounts. This method is not loved by accountants as it often leads to errors, and it is more onerous to determine if the debits and credits match. By entering an amount directly in the Chart of Accounts for the specific account, QBO automatically makes an entry to "opening balance equity". The balance in the opening balance equity account should always be $0.00, unless there is an exceptional circumstance. Using this method does not always achieve this result as it easy to miss a balance or enter it incorrectly.*
>
> ⇨ ***Enter opening balances via a Journal Entry****: This method is preferable as, since your debits and credits have to match, there is no "opening balance equity" account. Rather every balance is specifically allocated to an account in a Journal Entry. This is the option we will use below.*

To create a Journal Entry, first you must determine the closing balances from the date of transfer and whether they are debits or credits. Generally speaking:

- Assets and Expenses are <u>Debits</u>
- Liabilities, equity, and revenues are <u>Credits</u>

Note that there are some amounts known as "contra" accounts that are negative assets or liabilities, e.g., accumulated depreciation, allowance for doubtful accounts (AFDA), and sales returns.

The starting point for your Journal Entry is the Balance Sheet at the previous year end. A year end date is recommended as the date of transition so that you know exactly what your previous year end balances are; you can then compare them to Financial Statements and tax returns, which makes it much easier when doing future year end reporting and tax returns.

If you are transitioning from existing accounting software or spreadsheet and already have a Balance Sheet:

1. Generate a Balance Sheet at the last year end from your previous accounting software.
2. Ensure that the accounts that are on the Balance Sheet are found on the Chart of Accounts. If not, create them in their appropriate categories.
3. Click on <+ New> (from the Left-hand Navigation Bar).
4. Select **Journal Entry** which can be found under the **OTHER** column.
5. Enter the date of the Journal Entry, which is your previous year end.
6. Enter the assets as debits.
7. Enter the liabilities and equity amounts as credits.
8. If you have a negative asset or liability, enter it as a credit or debit respectively.

Note that there are some opening balances in QBO that require additional attention:

- **Customers** When entering Accounts Receivable, you are required to enter a Customer. Make sure each Customer has been created in the **Sales >** (or **Invoicing >**) section of QBO. When entering the Journal Entry, you would enter each individual Accounts Receivable balance along with the Customer.
- **Accounts Receivable** If you have a large customer list, you can also import the balances for each Customer which QBO would post to "opening balance equity". In this case, the total Accounts Receivable can be entered as a debit to opening balance equity. Make sure this total is exactly equal to the amount imported in the Accounts Receivable.
- **Accounts payable** The same process for Accounts Receivable applies to Accounts Payable.
- **Inventory** is also similar. If you are entering or importing each item into QBO, then the same process for opening balance equity applies.

If you are transitioning from a spreadsheet and do not have a Balance Sheet you can create one, in a spreadsheet, at your previous year end, by assigning the amounts as follows:

Assets

- Bank Balance is total amount in your business bank account(s).
- Accounts Receivable are amounts owing from Customers.
- Fixed Assets include items such as computer equipment, furniture etc.
- Any other asset accounts, itemized.

Liabilities

- Credit card include the total credit card balances owing.
- Loan balances including any loans or line of credit amounts.
- Accounts Payable include amounts owing to Suppliers.
- Any other liability accounts, itemized.

Owner's Equity

- Difference between total assets and total liabilities.

Once you have created your Balance Sheet:

1. Click on <+ New> (found on the Left-hand Navigation Bar).
2. Select **Journal Entry**, which can be found under the **OTHER** column.
3. Enter the date of the Journal Entry , which is your previous year end.
4. Enter the assets as debits.
5. Enter the liabilities and equity amounts as credits.

How To Generate Your Opening Balance (Balance Sheet) Report

Once you have entered your opening balances, go to Reports from the **Left-hand Navigation Bar** in QBO and select **Balance Sheet**. Choose the last year end date and **<Run report>**. You will then see all the balances that you have entered. Each balance should correspond to the amounts from your year end Balance Sheet and the opening balance equity account should be $0.00.

Entering your opening balances is a necessary process that must be undertaken by anyone transitioning to QBO. The good news is that with some guidance it doesn't have to be overwhelming.

ABOUT THE AUTHOR

My name is Ronika Khanna. I am a Chartered Professional Accountant (CPA), Chartered Accountant (CA), and Chartered Financial Analyst (CFA), and the founder of Montreal Financial, an accounting, tax and financial consulting services business. After having worked as an accounting professional for several companies, both in Canada and Bermuda, including with PricewaterhouseCoopers (PwC) and ING Risk Management Limited, I decided to launch my own business, focusing primarily on the accounting, tax, and financial needs of small business owners, start-ups, and independent contractors.

I have helped numerous small businesses with their financial, accounting, and tax reporting over the years, which has allowed them to run their businesses more effectively and profitably. I have also taught many of them to set up and use Quickbooks Online which has allowed them to better understand their businesses and be more confident about doing their own accounting.

I would love for us to connect, which you can do by subscribing to my biweekly newsletter, where I discuss topics of interest to small businesses, provide tax and QuickBooks tips and links to my latest articles. You can also email me at ronika@montrealfinancial.ca.

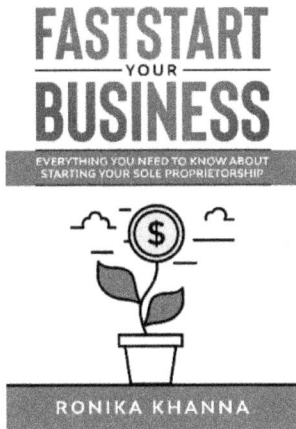

Starting a business from nothing is an intimidating prospect! Launch your enterprise with confidence using this step-by-step guide to starting your Canadian sole proprietorship. Learn about the registration process, setting up your bank accounts, HST & GST, accounting, invoicing, and, of course, how to pay yourself. Starting your own business doesn't mean you have to start it all on your own. Find the answers you need in this handy, easy-to-read book.

Starting a business or becoming self-employed opens up a whole new world of tax considerations. This book will guide you through the fundamentals to ensure that you pay the taxes you need to but no more than that. In learning about the different types of tax and the sorts of deductions that businesses are entitled to you can have a better understanding of your small business tax and save time and money.

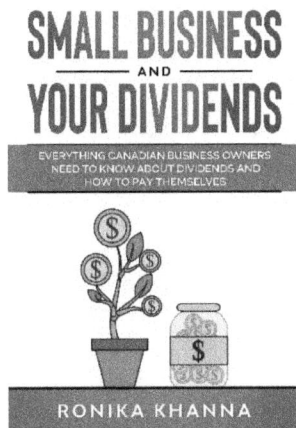

For small business owners, administrators, and bookkeepers, this book will help you to understand everything you need to know about paying yourself using small business dividends. Step by step instructions guide you through preparing and submitting your own tax filings to the government.

www.ingramcontent.com/pod-product-compliance
Lightning Source LLC
Chambersburg PA
CBHW051752200326
41597CB00025B/4521